SELL OR DON'T EAT

HOW SELLING FROM THE SOUL WILL KEEP FOOD ON YOUR TABLE

DON W. LONG

To the most amazing parents who taught me so many things over my lifetime. To my mother, Joan Shoe, whose love and belief in me caused me to soar beyond where I thought I could go. Additionally, to both of my dads, Wesley Long and Jimmy Shoe, who taught me the value of hard work and never giving up. From the farmhouse to the golf course, I learned to take care of the small things that mattered so that the larger things in life would take care of themselves. Love all of you so much. Thank you.

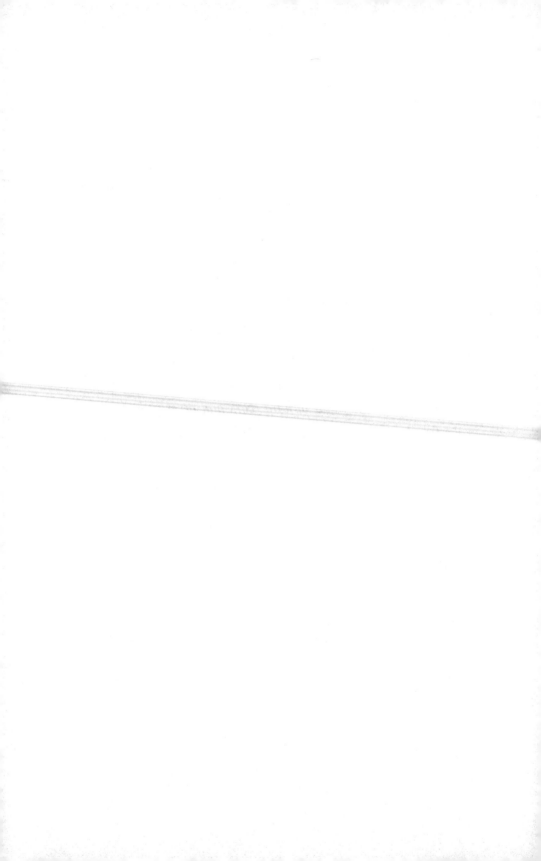

Free Gift

As a way of saying "Thank-You" to my Readers I have a special gift for you. Click the link below and download your Free Gift, *7 Simple Steps to Double Your Sales*!

Visit **https://DonWLong.com/freegift/** to receive your free gift.

Table of Contents

Out of this endeavor, within 36 months, we grew another multimillion-dollar business within this first business, and sold it in 2000–2001.

In 2010, I made the best and largest purchase of my career. I decided to move the corporate office to the Raleigh-Durham area.

I rebranded the company and doubled sales in one part of the business. From 2010 to 2017, the company was in the top one percent in four of the top five key metrics, and in the top 1,000 of 96,342 companies in our space.

In addition, our real estate investment property doubled in value from 2012 to 2017.

All of this happened because of the principles I'm sharing with you in this book.

The most important thing I can tell you is this...*you are enough.* Somewhere in your mind, your heart, your soul, or your past, there is a voice whispering to you, telling you that you're not enough.

The reality is you are. You may not know it yet, but your DNA contains all the elements, the patterns, the divine design that destined you to be a success.

It's been there all along; all you need to do is learn how to tap into it. It's not difficult to do, but it will require a commitment— not to me, but to yourself.

You already have the three things you need to succeed. The first is DNA, which is the pattern that defines what kind of person you are, what you look like, what your potential is, and what you will and can be.

The second is the ability to transform, grow, change, and evolve. None of those are conscious. You will transform, grow, and change regardless of what you do. You're not the baby you once were, and until you die, you will keep growing and changing. How much you transform, how much you grow, and how you use your hidden potential depends on your heart and soul.

The third is choice. You can choose to change, to grow, to succeed, or not. If you choose to change, I will help you.

Selling from the Soul isn't about selling techniques as much as it's about becoming the kind of person people want to buy from and do business with.

Selling from the soul and being a salesperson are as different as knowing the path and walking the path. The difference is this…the first is who you are, the second is something you do.

When you don't have to "put on" your sales personality, you're able to connect and sell 24/7 because you're helping people, not pressuring them into buying.

I want you to:

- See yourself.

- See the way you see selling.

- Sell because you have influence, without manipulation or pressure.

There are no gimmicks in this book. There are no secrets. There are no silver bullets.

What I'm about to tell you is freely available in different articles around the internet, in other books, and from almost any webinar you might want to attend.

These are proven practices, but because they take some work, most people don't want to follow them. They can't or don't want to change, or they're afraid or uncertain about change. They don't think they're enough, or that people will buy from them if they don't act a certain way. That's simply not true.

The one thing people value more than looks, charisma, or personality is authenticity.

Your customer or client won't care what you look like, how well you speak, what kind of car you drive, or how young or old you are if they believe you're the real deal.

You must illustrate that you are trustworthy, authentic, and you have their best interest at heart. I guarantee that.

What I have to offer you is my thirty-five years of experience and all it took for me to learn that one simple truth.

We learn by failing, but if you don't want to spend a lot of time failing, it's possible to learn a lot from the mistakes of others.

Hence, I offer my mistakes, lessons, insights, and support.

I expect you to do the heavy lifting. It's your life after all. By "heavy lifting," I mean it's up to you to do the exercises, keep a journal, find a mentor, coach, friend, or spouse who can help keep you accountable, and then, as they say, "rinse and repeat."

I will unpack as much as I can in the following pages, but if you want to become the best salesperson you can be, you'll have to read and apply the knowledge I share. Changing how you sell now is an investment you make in yourself.

In one year, three years, five years, or however long you live, you'll be that much older no matter what you do. No matter what decisions you make about this book, the *Selling from the Soul* course, your sales career, or your life, you'll still be one year, three years, or five years older.

It only makes sense to find yourself down that path, not just older, but wiser.

Here I give you your chance.

Getting the Most Out of This Book

You can't change what you can't measure. To get the most out of this book, you'll need to buy a journal or notebook and document your progress, failures, successes, questions, and challenges.

Review your entries on a weekly basis.

It's the best way to see what you've learned and where you're going, and keep track of your goals. Any notebook will do, or I like having a journal dedicated for different projects to keep up with. You can also contact me at https://DonWLong.com.

1

Influence: The Power of You

The first requirement for being an influential person is knowing your-self."

— Dr. Karen Keller

Selling well is about one thing…Influence.

People follow, listen, admire, change, give, and buy from those who have influence with them. However, influence is more than getting people to go along with your suggestions.

True influence creates an internal shift and change in a person's mindset. When we influence people, we gain an internal commitment from them, independent of external consequences.

When people are influenced, versus commanded, manipulated, or expected to do something other people do, buy, think, or act, they are truly being positively influenced.

This positive influence is because they have changed from the inside out. They don't do something because they're being forced to change or because they're told, ordered, or manipulated to do so.

They take action because they want to.

The world's most influential people don't merely change other's behavior; they shift their mindsets. That's real power.

For instance, let's say I have an employee who doesn't treat clients well as our company culture requires. I can say, "Do this, or you'll get fired." Or I can say, "Let me show you why treating our clients is important to your success and mine."

The employee who is commanded to treat our clients well will do so, but only when he or she thinks I'm watching them.

It will be stressful for us both, and worse, our clients will know it's not genuine when they do receive the fake treatment.

However, if I can influence my employee and create an internal shift in them so their behavior changes from the inside out, then I've done more than change their behavior. I've changed their attitude.

You may be one of a dozen salespeople on your team or the lone salesperson at a small company. What matters is that you become the best influencer you can be to become the best salesperson you can be.

Over the course of this book, you'll find me moving from the term "salesperson" to the term "influencer."

That's really what a great salesperson does—they influence their client to make an informed choice that will solve, eliminate, or reduce the client's pain or problem as effectively and efficiently as possible.

That's kind of a different take on "sales" which may be unfamiliar to of you; however, it's what *Selling from the Soul* is all about.

It's the most powerful way to connect with people and to help them make an informed decision about your product or service.

I guarantee if you take the time to understand, implement, and practice what I'm am sharing in this book, you will see financial and personal success beyond what you could ever imagine—all from becoming an "influencer" rather than a salesperson.

I'm not the only one who believes this.

The world's most powerful leaders, business people, and innovators know the key characteristic of their success is their ability to be influential.

Influence means to "have an effect on the character, development, or behavior of someone or something."

Influence is the most powerful force in the world—it opens the doors that wealth, success, and even fame can't.

There are millions of people, many of whom labor in places that seem insignificant to others, then seemingly out of nowhere they gain influence and change the world, either publicly, or in their chosen fields.

They can do so because they have learned how to influence others. If they can do it, so can you.

It takes these qualities:[i]

- Knowing your personality and uniqueness

- Being alive, physically, mentally, emotionally, and psychologically

- Embracing your strengths, uniqueness, and authenticity

- Trust in what you're selling, who you are, and what you believe

Have you ever noticed that leaders, influencers, and trendsetters aren't the people who fit in or act like everyone else? Often they are outliers and different.

They think differently, they act differently, and they engage differently. They're not different because it's a gimmick.

They're different because they're being their authentic selves.

They know what they want, who they are, and what it will take to get where they want to be. They know what makes them feel alive, and they go after it.

They don't have the time or the energy to be concerned with what others think of them. They're busy thinking positively about who and what they are, and achieving their goals.

When we begin to understand, consistently embrace, and be our authentic selves, we begin to come alive, and we begin to develop influence with those around us.

What about you? Who are you? What makes you come alive?

I don't mean what makes you feel good. I mean what excites you and makes you want to jump out of bed in the morning and live, work, and engage with the world around you?

For me, that means focusing on my children, my family, and a desire to build wealth for myself, my family, and others, including generations to come. I feel most alive when I'm growing and contributing to my family, my community, and the world. By growth I mean finding, searching for, discovering, applying, and sharing new golden nuggets of wisdom by reading new books and new ideas—that jazzes me.

The deep study to unearth those treasures of wisdom helps me feel alive. Finally, being able to give away to others what has worked for me in my family and business life, and then to see how my experiences trans-form the lives of others, also makes me want to get up and get going every morning. It's absolutely wonderful. Knowing what makes me come alive is what helps me set and focus my day-to-day and long-term goals.

Finding what makes you come alive will do the same for you.

Your goals may be different than mine, or your parents, spouse, friends or family, which is completely okay. They're your goals and they have the power to change your life if you'll let them. That's a fact.

Researchers have found that people who want to make a big change in their lives, either to lose weight, stop smoking, get a better job, finish college, etc., always do better when they know why *they* want to change (motivated by children, spouse, marriage, health. etc.).

That 'why' is the motivation that lasts. If you're doing something—anything—because someone else wants you to do it, you won't be able to sustain yourself through the failures, setbacks, and tough times that change will bring.

You have to know and must want to know your own why. Your 'why' might be so you can spend more time with your family. You may have a personal income goal. It might be a desire to build your company to the level where it can go public, or where you can have more time to travel regularly.

I know people whose *why* factor is the desire to be financially independent so they can retire early and travel. Whatever your why factor is, it must be a strong incentive you can clearly define.

For some, that may mean having a photo of your why (family, new home, new car, or whatever it is).

For others, it may mean writing out the *why*, for example, "Following this diet will make me healthier so I'll have energy and enjoy the time when my kids graduate high school and college, and get married."

It doesn't have to be a manifesto, but it should be something you can look at or read every day to remind you why you're doing what you're doing.

Make it one sentence you can write on an index card—the simpler, the better. That's the first step in finding your why.

Discover what makes you feel alive. Discover your unique skills, strengths, and weaknesses, and work with what you have and who you are.

Don't think about *how* to influence others.

That comes naturally as you begin to understand your strengths, weaknesses, talents, skills, and personality. That awareness and knowledge doesn't happen overnight, and it never ends. It's a lifelong journey, one that just improves as you embrace and practice it.

Being alive isn't just something you do for yourself, so you feel good when you wake up in the morning. People love to be around fully alive people. Be alive for yourself first, then do it because it helps you connect with others.

Life is different when you're present, engaged, and excited about it.

Unpacking Your Uniqueness

You probably already know that no two human beings have the same fingerprints. Even identical twins have non-identical fingerprints. Even dogs have different nose prints! That's right. No two nose prints are alike.

And snowflakes—as much as they seem the same to the untrained eye, there are no two snowflakes alike either. So, if you're thinking you don't have anything different, let alone unique, to offer the world, you're wrong.

You came into this world uniquely you. Everything about you is unique, from your voice, your laugh, the way you think, to how you see and respond to the world.

You just have to find and unpack that uniqueness in a way that attracts people to you, and then allows you to influence them in a healthy, uniquely "you" kind of way.

I want you to do something to help you now.

Set this book down for a minute and look in the mirror. Think about how you look, walk, talk, and how you carry yourself. Now think about your spouse, or a significant other, or your best friend.

What makes them unique? Is it their personality? Their sense of humor? The way they respond when someone needs something? What is it you admire about them? What do you like? What makes them have influence with you? Just be aware of what you see, think, and feel about yourself, and those you admire or are surrounded by.

What makes you unique? It might be something as simple as your ability to:

- Empathize with people's needs while in conversation.

- See other people's needs in your product or service.

- Connect with people at a deep level.

- Stay optimistic.

- Use your intuition or insight.

- Listen to others and really hear what they're saying

- Focus on the positive things, not the negative.

If you can't figure out what makes you unique, ask your spouse or a close friend—someone who knows you really well. They'll help you with your list.

Knowing what makes you unique will help you move forward. It's all about action. It's all about you finding a way to put yourself out there, so to speak.

Your influence ultimately depends on how well you know yourself, your strengths, and your weaknesses.

By understanding who you are, what you can do, and what you're capable of, you're essentially taking an inventory of your personal resources.

Until you know what you have, or don't have, what your strengths, talents, and unique qualities are, you can't influence anyone to the degree of changing the world.

What Qualities Make a Great Salesperson?

We're all "salespeople." We all "sell" ourselves every day. We sell our spouse on doing something they may not want to do.

We sell our children on choosing to obey our rules. We sell our friends on going to one restaurant over another or helping us with something we need assistance with.

Okay, maybe those things aren't so much "selling" someone on doing something as they are about persuading someone to do or choose one thing over another.

Some of us are better persuaders than others. We call people that are good persuaders "salespeople," but what are they really doing? The good ones are "selling," but the experts are "influencing."

Selling is about influence. I want to hit this concept hard and to come out of the gate with the most powerful thing you'll ever learn about selling.

Selling is about building a true and honest rapport with people as quickly as possible. Selling is about people feeling that you're not trying to take advantage of them, but that you're authentic and you are there to help them solve a real problem they have.

They should realize you're well versed in what you're talking about and that you're attempting to provide a great and superior service and/or product to them with a superior result.

Influencing Skills

Truly excellent influencing skills require a healthy combination of interpersonal, communication, presentation, and assertiveness techniques.

Even more important than those skills is authenticity.

Authenticity is the greatest element in sales. You know, it doesn't matter for everyone because some people are more gullible than others. Let me say this...most people, whether they're a mom, a student, an engineer, or a business owner, sooner or later will have enough life experience to know the difference between real and fake.

This instinct is honed by some people at a younger age than others, while others never learn.

I know people who wouldn't represent the prototypical salesperson in my industry, and I also have two or three people that sell really well at our company, who fit the prototypical— maybe two of them—and then the other two wouldn't.

The first step in this process would be you being real and authentic, first and foremost, with yourself.

Whatever you are, you are.

That's a deep statement and you need to grab that. Your gifts, talents, and abilities have certain things within your creativity mix that have come from the creator that are his fingerprint on your life and can be monetized and will help you create wealth.

Some of that, no matter what you do, requires influence. Would you agree with that?

Influence is simply gaining people's trust. The first step in this is to actually be you. Sooner or later, you will.

Most of your clients and most of the people you're seeking to sell your particular service or product to will know whether you're fake or not.

Selling from the Soul is about discovering who you are, identifying your strengths, skills, talents, and abilities, and learning how to become the kind of authentic person who can not only influence others, but be better, happier, and more content.

Let's get started.

2

Build on Your Strengths

Knowing others is intelligence; knowing yourself is true wisdom. Mastering others is strength; mastering yourself is true power."

– Tao Te Ching

If you're like most of us, you've heard that you should "work on your weaknesses, as your strengths are already fine." That's bad advice.

Your weaknesses will always be weaknesses. To focus on what you don't do well is like telling a fish it needs to improve its tree climbing skills.

Find and focus on your strengths. There's nothing wrong with working on areas of your life you'd like to improve on, however, you have to find, focus, and build on what you're good at.

Build on Your Strengths

I'm not a tech-savvy person. I don't have the patience for it. I can manage email, web searches, and the basics, but when it comes to different programs, and all the technical stuff, I have a staff person I've hired to take care of those things.

My IT person is good with IT. I'm not. IT is not my strength.

I'm good with people, sales, managing my teams, and other things I do. I know in school we were all encouraged to work on our weaknesses, not on our strengths, but that's counterproductive.

First, if you're not good at something, is it a weakness? And if you're good at something, is it a strength? Actually, it's not that simple.

J.D. Meier, the best-selling author of *Getting Results the Agile Way* puts it like this, "Strengths are your dominant thinking, feeling, and doing patterns. They're the things that come naturally for you. You grow stronger when you spend time in your strengths. A weakness drains you, and no matter how much you work at it, you don't really improve."[ii]

I could take some classes. I could spend time learning how to be better at certain things, but that would take time away from the things I'm really good at.

I like meeting people, running my businesses, and selling. I can achieve far more by focusing on my strengths.

There are strengths, then there are skills, which are different from strengths.

For instance, we all started life unable to crawl. Then we learned to crawl, then to walk, then to run. Those are all skills.

Some people are really fast, and running is something that comes naturally to them. Good runners enjoy running and the more time they spend running the better they get at it. For them, it's a strength. They grow stronger when they're spending time in their strength.

For the rest of us? We can run every day and never come close to achieving the strength of a naturally gifted or talented runner.

It's the same with sports, with business, with driving a car, with any skill. We can improve to a point, but then we often hit a wall, or worse, we stop enjoying it. We may even resent being expected to do it.

I've seen this with salespeople who make better sales team managers than salespeople, and vice versa. Just because someone is an incredible salesperson doesn't mean they should be managing salespeople if it's not one of their strengths.

I've seen successful salespeople who were pulled into management and asked to mentor other salespeople who were destined to fail. Why? They weren't strong managers. They tried and found they didn't like it, didn't get it, and didn't do it well. Point being, don't work on your weaknesses.

You'll never rise to your star level and where you are designed to be by focusing on your weakness. Let me add a caveat, however. I didn't say not to work on moral issues, character flaws, or areas where you're lacking personal or ethical problems. That's different.

If you have any issues in these areas, do what's needed to get victory over them. Keep working on them—even if it takes a lifetime. The things I'm talking about are minimizing those physical or work-related *skill sets you're* not good at. For example, if you're not good at organization, outsource this responsibility.

You can also focus on creating enough income through the process of adding clients to *bridge the things you're not good at*. Many small business owners find themselves wearing many hats, doing things they're really not good at in the beginning.

Owners end up doing their own marketing, updating their website, and bookkeeping. If you're in that situation, then find the most critical skills and outsource those first. For instance, accounting, bookkeeping, taxes, or marketing.

Then work on increasing your income through what you're good at so you can build a successful business. Eventually you can bridge across the things you're not that good at, and work only in your strength zones. This is what you *should* be doing.

Focus on getting better at what you do love and can do well, like talking, listening, engaging, and selling. If you don't know what your strengths are, take a few personality tests to find out. Talk to your family and friends. Discover yourself. You can do this through a variety of ways, including personality testing, counseling, books, self-help courses, coaching, or finding a good mentor who can spot and help nurture those strengths in you.

I'm a big believer in beginning your search with the Marston's DISC Profile. There are many other personality assessments you can take, such as Strengths Finder and the Myers-Briggs Type Indicator, but I prefer the Marston's DISC.

You can add others as you explore. Every test you take should give you both a list of strengths and a list of weaknesses. When I teach the people who are closest to me, those to whom I speak and those whom I mentor, I tell them this:

In any season in which you find yourself up against the wall, always know your strengths and your weaknesses.

Why? Imagine being challenged to perform a task, any task. The first thing a leader does is inventory their resources.

What do they have access to that can help them accomplish the task? Knowing your strengths and weaknesses, taking inventory of who you are means seizing control of all your assets. Knowing your strengths and weaknesses will help you set goals, as well as make better decisions based on that information.

Maybe your strength is your work ethic. You feel responsible for yourself and get the job done no matter what it takes. You're not afraid of hard work or long hours. Other words that describe personal strengths include:

Accurate: You're detail oriented. The more you do it, the better you get. Accuracy is a critical skill that many teams need—and one that's hard to find. Doing a job properly, accurately, and thoroughly saves time in the long run.

Action-oriented: You're not afraid to move forward. You have a strong sense of immediacy, focusing on the task at hand

and seeing it through to fruition. You complete the tasks you commit to.

Adventurous: You're willing to take risks. You're bold and courageous. You're rarely influenced by other people or by the norms of society and the status quo. You tend not to worry about others and expect each person on your team to be responsible for themselves. You're a nonconformist.

Ambitious: You have high expectations and the tenacity to stop at nothing to achieve your goals. You focus on execution, not excuses. "On average, ambitious people attain higher levels of education and income, build more prestigious careers, and report higher overall levels of life satisfaction," says Neel Burton, psychiatrist and author of *Heaven and Hell: The Psychology of the Emotions*. "Many of man's greatest achievements are the products, or accidents, of their ambition."

Analytical: You tend to search for reasons and causes. You think about all the factors that might affect a situation. You dissect ideas and examine them carefully.

Appreciative: You're able to see and appreciate other's abilities, skills, and contributions.

Artistic: You see the form, function, and beauty in things around you, and can incorporate them into solutions, business, and your interactions with others.

Athletic: You have confidence in your body and your physical abilities. You're a team player with a healthy competitiveness and good self-discipline—valuable assets to any team.

Creative: You can devise multiple solutions to any given problem. You think outside the box, looking for solutions from different disciplines. You're not limited by doing things the way they've always been done. You entertain multiple interests and passions. You take the time to explore new cultures, places, and ideas.

Determined: You may not be the smartest, fastest, strongest, or best, but you tend to succeed because of your determination. You don't stop until you've reached your goals. You tend to go farther than most people expect because you find ways around obstacles, challenges, and failures.

Dedicated: You're on fire, purpose-driven, and devoted to the task at hand. You're often the first to arrive at work and the last to leave. You believe fiercely and strongly in what you do and are naturally passionate about whatever you pursue.

Disciplined: You get stuff done. You order and plan, and as a result are able to create systematic ways to accomplish your goals.

Enthusiastic: You feel and share strong excitement or an active interest in the things you enjoy. You bring energy and excitement to your work and your relationships.

Patient: You can bear provocation, annoyance, misfortune, and pain without complaint, loss of temper, or irritation. You're able to suppress restlessness or annoyance when you're confronted with delays. Patience is a virtue you can work on, and is personality related. It's not a skill that can be learned. You can, however, learn to hide your impatience.

Respectful: You are able to see and celebrate the value in yourself and others. Being respectful is one of the six core strengths required for healthy emotional development. According to Dr. Bruce Duncan Perry, it requires the emotional, social, and cognitive maturity that comes from developing the other five core strengths (attachment, self-regulation, affiliation, awareness, and tolerance).[iii]

Trustworthy: To be seen as trustworthy, one of the most valuable strengths, you need warmth and competence. You're consistent, authentic, compassionate, kind, resourceful, humble, and available, and you have integrity. You are a connector—you connect people with each other in ways that benefit all.[iv]

Here are some other abilities that employers want to see:

Be a strong leader: Do you know what it means to be a leader? Do you know how to lead? Do you know how to delegate?

Have problem solving and decision making skills: Do you understand the decision-making process? Can you make decisions wisely and quickly? Are you willing and able to accept responsibility for your decisions, or do you blame others, or circumstances, when you make the wrong decision?

Communicate effectively: Can you express yourself well? Can you convey your ideas, goals, thoughts, and information clearly? Is your writing easily understood by others? Can you summarize and structure information in a way that makes sense and contributes to the understanding of a project? Can you effectively represent the company brand and culture?

Be a team player: Can you work well with people you don't like to accomplish a task or goal? Do you communicate well with all personality types?

Be a quick learner: Do you pick things up quickly? Or do you struggle to learn new skills? Do you like learning? Can you stick with something even if it's challenging?

Be tolerant: Do you deal well with stress and change? If you're not naturally patient, can you hide your impatience?

Have a strong work ethic: Do you do your job without being prodded by colleagues or supervisors? Do you do what you were hired for and then some, or do you do the minimum you need to get by?

Take initiative: Do you look for things to do when you finish a task, or do you wait around for someone to tell you what to do next? Do you take the initiative and look for ways to improve, act, or respond to situations?

Be tech savvy: Do you know your way around a computer? Can you troubleshoot basic problems? Do you know how to use basic software, like email, the Microsoft Office suite, and Google Docs?

You may have other strengths that are not listed here. Write down three of your strengths. They may be your people skills, your ability to network, your positive attitude, or your work ethic—just pick three.

Now, meditate on those three strengths. Meditation means to "ponder, converse with oneself, and hence aloud, to utter, commune, declare, meditate, muse, pray, speak, talk"—in other words, sit with the thought about what your strengths are, where and how you use them, how you *could* use them.

Think about what roles they play in who you are and what you want to become. Write those thoughts and any questions or insights you have in your journal. That way you can go back to them later and see what you've learned or implemented in your life based on your meditation. This is not an easy or lightweight exercise. This changes you if and when you act on it.

Take a Lesson from Navy SEAL Training

Why is it so critical to meditate? It helps you develop "mental toughness." When I think about mental toughness, the first thing that comes to mind is Navy SEAL training. The beginning is a six-week vetting process of sorts. At the end of the six weeks comes a period called "Hell Week," when recruits get about four hours of sleep over a sixty-hour period. They spend long amounts of time in cold water and covered with sand. It's brutal. It was so tough that about 76 percent of the recruits gave up and quit. That kind of failure rate cost the Navy a lot of money.

So, they brought in a psychologist, Dr. Eric Potterat. He didn't look at the training or the physical demands. He focused on the mental toughness training and made four changes.

Remarkably, the graduation rate increased by 50 percent.

Potterat implemented a practice called "mindfulness." Mindfulness isn't New Age-y. It's a scientifically-based model of thinking. It's the psychological process of bringing your attention to what is happening to you mentally, emotionally, and physically, and in the present moment.

It's powerful stuff. "When we allow our attention to be captured by fear," says Potterat, "our level of fear grows. But if we swing our attentional spotlight to focus on something else, our brains will respond in kind."

Here are the four changes that Potterat had the SEALs make that you should make as well.

Focus on Right Now

Don't think about anything other than what is happening right now. Just get to the end of the current task. Don't think about dinner, or what you have to do tomorrow, or your relationship, or what you need to do after work.

If you're doing a twenty-mile run, focus on finishing the twenty-mile run. If you're making twenty cold calls, focus on the calls, not on what will happen afterward. If you find your mind wandering, don't be critical, just notice it and go back to focusing on what you're feeling, what's happening, what's going on in the exact moment where you are. It takes practice, but you can do it. The more you do it, the easier it becomes—it's like strengthening your brain muscles.

You can break this down even further.

If you have twenty calls to make, focus on the next call. Focus on the number. Then focus on the person who answers. Focus on the next step, then the next. Concentrate on that call. Chunk the task into micro-steps. Focus on each micro-step until you complete it. Then keep going until you finish the larger goal.

Imagine How Good It Will Feel to Succeed

Think about all your past successes. Taste them, smell them, hear them. Bring all your sensory memory about them to mind.

Now transfer those feelings to how good it will feel to complete your current task. Feel these things with each micro-step. Tell yourself how good it will feel to finish that step. Keep going. Each micro-step is a mini-victory that will help motivate you to complete the larger goal.

Breathe Deeply

When you get frustrated, drained, angry or depressed at your inability to finish a challenge or difficult task, you'll start to shallow breathe. It's just how the body works.

Those feelings and shallow breathing combine to create a sense of panic in a part of the brain called the amygdala.

Once the amygdala kicks into overdrive, it's almost impossible to overcome feelings of fear and panic, unless you breathe, and breathe deeply.

When you intentionally breathe deeply, into your diaphragm, you flood your body with oxygen.

This stops the panic and reduces cortisol, a stress hormone.

Here's a quick, easy breathing exercise. Inhale into the diaphragm (see your lower belly, not your stomach rise) for a count of six. Hold for a count of two. Then exhale for a count of six. Repeat this cycle three times.

Cheer for Yourself

Flip the switch on those negative thoughts. Instead of saying to yourself, "I can't do this. I'll never be able to make these calls, pitch this client, close this sale," cheer yourself on. Flip the negative thoughts and change them into positive ones. Say, "I can do this. I will do this. I can make these calls. I can close this sale. I can deliver a great pitch." Focus on that next micro-step, the next problem, and tell yourself you can get there and you will.

If the Navy SEALs can use these tactics to complete some of the most physically and mentally grueling tasks imaginable, you can use them to tackle any challenge you have as well. If you get panic attacks, doubt yourself, fear or dread the task in front of you, apply these steps. This approach works best when you know yourself, and know and focus on your strengths.

Focus on Your Strengths

Realize that your strengths are tied to your God-given gifts. They're literally in your DNA. You were created with them. They're yours. Practice improving your strengths weekly. If it's more helpful, practice one strength at a time. As you strengthen your strengths, you'll be more in control of them. Ultimately, it's your top three strengths that will help you start accomplishing your goals. How? Let's say, for example, that your strength is building a client base. How would you improve that strength? You might work on:

- Develop your LinkedIn profile to attract more people into your network.

- Identify three new people on LinkedIn, through the networks of people you know, whom you haven't met.

- Reach out to these new people, sharing with them the fact that you have mutual connections in your networks, to start building out your network with new opportunities.

Discover Your Personality DNA

Your strengths, weaknesses, and uniqueness are what I call your *personality* DNA. DNA is a code that carries the instructions for the growth, development, functioning, and reproduction of all living organisms. It's like a how-to manual for everything to do with your body—from your eye color, to how tall or short you are, to your body type, muscular development, and even how many teeth you have. It's the blueprint, the thing that makes you who you are, right down to your personality.

I consider a person's personality DNA to be the gifts, talents, and abilities that were put into them by the Creator before they were born. These things are innate. Just like fingerprints, no two human beings are exactly alike. We all have a blend of strengths, talents, abilities, and life experiences that make us uniquely and wonderful us. Even identical twins have different fingerprints and different personalities. The sooner you learn what your DNA entails, the closer you are to fulfilling your potential and the things you're destined for.

Your strengths, oddly enough, are the things that come easily to you, or that other people see as something you can do that they can't. We're often blind to our own talents, and that's what makes them hard to identify. Maybe you find it easy and natural to strike up a conversation with a stranger. That's a talent and ability and part of your DNA. I always tell people, if you look at your strengths, you'll find your strengths are always tied to your ability and talent.

Like I said, taking a personality test makes the process of discovering your talents and abilities easier. Here are a few of the top tests:

DiSC profile: The DiSC profile is my favorite test. It's a nonjudgmental tool used for discussion of people's behavioral differences. DiSC measures your tendencies and preferences—your patterns of behavior. It doesn't measure your intelligence, aptitude, mental health, or values. DiSC profiles (D=dominance, I=influence, S=steadiness, C=conscientiousness) describe human behavior, or how you act or respond to others, in various situations. For example, the DiSC questionnaire asks about how you respond to challenges, how you influence others, how you respond to rules and procedures, and your preferred pace of activity. It doesn't measure every dimension of your personality but it does give accurate predictions about how you're likely to be in most social situations. All people have all four qualities but each person has a preferred DiSC-based preference based on their personality.

Myers-Briggs: The Myers-Briggs test has sixteen personalities and covers the "Big Five" personality traits of individuals: mind, energy, nature, tactics, and identity. With more than 26 million tests taken, it's one of the most popular personality quizzes online. It'll cover everything from your basic qualities to your romantic relationships to your workplace habits, strengths, and weaknesses.

Who Am I?: If you prefer something simple and visual, you'll like the Who Am I? Test. It's one of the most fun and useful personality quizzes you'll come across. Unlike most tests, it's less like question-and-answer and more like a "pick a photo that you think is pretty" test. It will definitely show how your character defines your outlook on and approach to life.

See My Personality Test: This test is more scientific and will show you if you're left or right brained. Designed by Ph.D. researchers to calculate your mental intelligence (IQ), it's just like the real deal.

There are at least a dozen tests out there, and these are just a sampling. Don't forget to take one (or more) emotional intelligence (EQ) tests too. These tests look at how well you function in society. For various reasons and thanks to a wide range of abilities, people with a high EQ tend to be more successful in life than those with lower EQ even if their classical IQ is average.[v] For most people, EQ is more important than IQ in attaining success in their lives and careers.

Our success as salespeople depends on our ability to read other people's signals and react appropriately to them. What factors are at play when people of high IQ fail and those of modest IQ succeed? Researchers tell us it's our EQ. How well you do in your life and career is determined by both IQ and EQ. In fact, psychologists generally agree that among the ingredients for success, IQ counts for roughly 10 percent (25 percent at best); the rest of your success depends on everything else, including EQ.

A study of Harvard graduates in business, law, medicine, and teaching showed a negative or zero correlation between an IQ indicator (entrance exam scores) and subsequent career success.[vi] Becoming emotionally competent is another factor in becoming influential and self-aware.

When you look at your list of strengths—specifically, the three that first jumped out at you—ask yourself, "What are these tied to? What talent and ability are these the foundation for that are good for me and good for my life?" (Your strengths will always be good for your life, by the way.)

I would then ask the deeper question because you're reading this book: "What is real to me in my talent and ability that these strengths tie to, and also, what will be monetizable?"

Some strengths and abilities, some of your talents, and some of your unique qualities are not always monetizable. If you love playing golf, but you're not good enough to be a pro at it, you might enjoy it, but it's really a hobby. You won't be good enough to make money from being a pro on tour, but you might be able to monetize some other aspect of your love for the game. Knowing where your strengths lie is critical to figuring out what to sell if you want to sell, and where to go next.

3

Authenticity

If you're your authentic self, you have no competition."

– Anonymous

Right now, there is an elite group of salespeople in the world. They are crushing it with their sales figures in all kinds of industries, from real estate to widgets. In a world where millions of salespeople are finding it impossible to make sales, these elite salespeople are consistently the top earners in their fields. Why? They understand that the emotional experience, the human connection, the relationship and the authenticity of who they are matters more to buyers than their product or service. Yes, you read that right.

Relationship matters to clients more than product or service. When we connect with others, when we believe that they understand us, care about us, and are genuinely concerned about us and our challenges, we trust them. When we trust people, when we believe they are authentic and real, we're more likely to share ourselves, our vulnerabilities, our challenges, and our concerns. And when a prospect trusts you, shares their real concerns and challenges, and turns to you for help—they're more likely to buy from you. At the core of that relationship and the ability to engage with people on that level is one thing—authenticity.

Authenticity and being real in what you do is more than important. It's critical. If you don't believe in your heart that what you're selling, and that can be anything from donuts to cars, is the best that you can sell to your customers, you'll fail. You may make the sale, but you've failed at sales because you're being inauthentic. You're betraying yourself, and you're betraying them. You've got to do your best to give your client a great experience through influencing them to trust you to buy what you're offering. That's true authenticity.

Authenticity is about you being real. You must be convinced that what you're attempting to provide to someone is superior and that it will give them a superior experience and superior results. If they feel that, they will buy from you. When I was selling Krispy Kreme donuts, the people who bought Krispy Kreme donuts from me were getting the freshest donuts they could get without walking in the store's doors themselves. It was the best experience they could have outside of driving down to the Krispy Kreme and standing in line.

If the experience is as good—sometimes—or better than the one they had with whatever other product or service they were buying from someone else, they will continue to buy from you. But, if it's not, they won't. It's really that simple.

You know, so much in life is based on levels of whether you win or lose. Not everything is black and white when it comes to answers, and developing your life. It takes time, it takes sowing, reaping, failing, feedback, and learning. But what I want you to realize is that in the business world, it's not like that. You may be learning and growing, but the bottom line is, either you make the sale or you don't, and you reap the consequences either way. If your life depends on creating income from sales, you need to learn how to influence people. You do this through your authentic voice, through understanding who you are and what you have to offer. And you need to believe in what you're trying to sell or influence people to buy.

I keep coming back to authenticity and its importance, because authenticity is the greatest element, and the most powerful skill any salesperson can have. As Brené Brown says, "Authenticity is a collection of choices that we have to make every day. It's about the choice to show up and be real. The choice to be honest. The choice to let our true selves be seen." When you're real, your buyer will feel it.

People are amazing creatures. We have sensors we're not even conscious of. These subconscious sensors help us pick up on things we aren't unaware of consciously, and help guide our decision-making process intuitively. It's what kept us alive when we were wandering the earth afraid of tigers, bears, and physical threats to our very being. It's called our "lizard brain," and it's the part of our brain that raises red flags and sets off alarm bells that say, "Danger! Warning! Run away!" Trust in others, in situations, and in ourselves is what kept our ancestors alive and it's still part of our survival instinct today. If you can't get your buyer to trust you, you're not going to make a sale. It's an inherent part of the sales process. If you're not authentic, people aren't going to trust you.

If you're uncomfortable being yourself, it will show in how you speak, move, act and engage with others, no matter how well you think you're disguising how you feel. You'll know, and your clients will know. They'll feel it. They may not know what they're feeling, but they will experience an unease, an uncomfortableness, a sense that something's not right, that you're being dishonest with them, even if you're telling the truth.

Our brains are sensitive to threats—and the biggest threat to a client is inauthenticity. Inauthenticity sets off alarms like nothing short of a saber-tooth tiger. It tells your potential client you want to steal their money, give them a bad product, and use and abuse them. You may not be thinking that, but that's what their lizard brain is telling them because something about you is "off." What they know is that something doesn't "feel right," and so they decline the sale, and worse, they reject you. No, it doesn't make sense, but that's how people operate. They want to feel safe, confident, and secure with both the salesperson and the product before they buy.

Think about a time when a salesperson didn't sound or seem authentic to you. Can you remember how it made you feel? Did you wonder if they were being honest about what they were selling? Did you buy from them?

Think about people you've met at school, work, or at social functions who seemed phony. Most of us will avoid people we perceive as phony or false unless we're forced to interact with them for some reason. We prefer to seek out friends and colleagues who are authentic, honest, and genuine. Clients are no different. They want to do business with people they like, trust, and perceive as authentic and trustworthy.

If you don't believe inside and out about what you're selling, you won't come across as authentic or real, and you're going to get chewed up and spit out. This is why so many good people in sales fail. A lot of times it's not that they can't learn to sell or aren't good at it; it's they don't believe in what they're selling, and/or they keep trying to be somebody else when they do it. Those are the two main reasons people fail in sales.

Believe in What You're Selling

If you don't believe in what you're selling, your clients know. The longer you try to sell something you don't believe in, the more evident it will become. Some people will buy, but most people will feel something is off or wrong and will walk away. They'll feel uneasy and/or suspicious. They won't know exactly why they don't want to buy from you, but they'll decide not to. Every sale you do make will feel like a struggle. And with each struggle, you'll start to hate what you're doing even more. That creates a vicious cycle you can't recover from without drastic actions.

Our authenticity is what attracts us to others, and others to us. But what is authenticity? It's more than just being truthful or honest about something. It's about being a psychologically mature and fully functioning human being. It means you're true to yourself, your beliefs, your values, and your boundaries. Authenticity is ultimately about showing up with the best you can bring, becoming the best version of yourself—those qualities that show healthy non-defensive functioning and psychological maturity. Those are the qualities we need to look for. To be authentic means:

- You're thoughtful. You're not the center of your universe. You think about others and express those thoughts verbally and with your actions.

- You know yourself. You know what motivates you, what your passions are, and are not, and you know what you like and don't like.

- You're able to express yourself, both your thoughts and feelings, easily and clearly.

- You embrace personal growth. You take critical feedback and learn from it. You're open to constructive criticism.

- You set good, healthy boundaries and you respect the boundaries of others.

- You may build castles in the air, but you don't live there. You have a realistic and reasonable perception of reality.

- You're more than just tolerant—you accept yourself and others for who they are and where they are in life.

- You're funny without being cruel or critical of others.

- You're true to yourself, your family, your community and your clients.[vii]

Be Someone People Want to be Around

When you're alive, you're engaged, interested, active, and involved. You listen. You care. You show that interest with both your words and actions. Here in the American South, we have a phrase to describe *not being alive*. We say a disengaged person is just "sitting there like a bump on a log." It means the person is not active, not engaged, not passionate, not anything. They're, well, just a "bump on a log."

No one likes to be around people they have to work hard to get to respond, to answer questions, or to engage in conversations. We all like people who come to the table, or party, or business, or whatever full of energy, positivity, and interest. We want to engage with people who are willing to take action to ensure they are contributing something in their interactions with others. If that's not you, and you want to be in sales, it's possible to develop those qualities, but you do have to be committed to personal growth and work to do so.

Fake never sells. When you're authentic you gain people's trust. Your strengths, gifts, talents, and abilities can be monetized because people trust you. You have to be convinced that what you're selling is valuable before you can convince others that it is. You don't have to be the best at what you do, you just have to be you. You are enough. If you don't have all the qualities listed above, don't worry. As long as you're on the path to self-improvement, you're developing them. At the end of the day, *Selling from the Soul* is all about being yourself, but it also requires you to take action to get in front of people. This book will cover all you need to do to take those actions, but first you need a firm foundation—and that foundation is authenticity.

If you're constantly looking outside yourself and obsessing over ways to be cool, powerful, liked, or well regarded, you're not being authentic. To be an authentic, unique person you have to know who and what you are. You can't know who or what you are without self-reflection, exploration, and working on getting to know yourself.

When we practice self-reflection, we experience less anxiety, more awareness, and more self-confidence. When you begin to discover and understand who you are and who you aren't, you stop worrying about others—what they have, who they are, and what they're good at—because you're confident enough to focus on your own strengths and uniqueness.

You learn you have nothing to hide or apologize for. You accept yourself. You value yourself. That gives you the freedom to be yourself. It's that confidence and freedom that people find so alluring and charismatic. The actions that flow from your acceptance of yourself, your passion, your strengths, and your uniqueness and mission in life create a strong energy and sense of purpose that so many others don't have. It's what attracts people to you and makes them want to buy from you, engage with you, and connect with you.

When you're authentic, you experience fewer emotional threats. You don't need to defend your ego, which means you're more able to listen to different points of view. You're able to be challenged by clients who doubt what you're saying and to learn. Authentic people thirst for truth. When you thirst for truth, you're open to truth. You want to find it, know it, and drink it in because it's what makes you feel most alive. This is what authenticity is all about.

Authentic people are open communicators. Honest communication is the foundation of authenticity. Authentic people are secure in who they are. Because they know who they are, and who they aren't, they are not threatened by accusations or the projections of others.

They don't leave people guessing about who they are, what they believe, or where they're coming from. They appreciate themselves, flaws and all, which makes them self-confident and secure, not cocky and conceited.

Non-authentic people are always defensive, sensitive to criticism, easily threatened and offended. It's like they have to be on the defensive all the time because they don't know what they need to protect because they don't know themselves. They are insecure and feel vulnerable all the time.

Self-confident people exude a sense of inner worth. They show a composure born of knowing who they are, are unashamed of their mistakes, and not afraid of their weaknesses. They have the courage to be who they really are.

People are attracted to authentic people because authentic people have a strong sense of character. They have integrity. They don't say things they don't mean, and they don't make promises they can't keep. They stay in a place of integrity in all their dealings, inside and outside of work. People trust them because they keep their word. They're consistent. They don't take themselves too seriously, because they know no one can steal who they are.

They don't need to sacrifice their integrity to win, or to prove something to others. Being authentic means not knowing all the answers, not being perfect, not understanding all the details of your buyer's industry or needs. It means being willing to be humble, matter of fact, and honest about what you don't know, can't provide, and don't understand. It's about being sincerely engaged to what your client's true issues are. They will begin to trust you, when you're willing to learn about their processes and products, by asking questions, and by educating yourself about what their real needs are, that your product or service might provide.

If all these descriptions are scaring you, don't let them. Authenticity is simply the state of being the best you. As you become more authentic through growth, there will be moments, days, or even weeks when you're "in the zone," and being, feeling, and experiencing true authenticity. Remember it's a journey, not a destination. Enjoy the process as you grow, and you will be amazed at how selling from soul will begin the flow of success in your life. You'll see how much of a sense of accomplishment you will have by simply learning to be you. And then you'll crash and find yourself in the valley where nothing is authentic, or good. Don't sweat it. The valley is where we learn, grow, and become better. Learn to accept the fact that self-growth and awareness is a process, not a destination. It gets easier. I promise.

4

Belief and Faith

As your faith is strengthened you will find that there is no longer the need to have a sense of control, that things will flow as they will, and that you will flow with them, to your great delight and benefit."

— Emmanuel Teney

Belief *and* faith are the power twins. Belief is the first step to developing your faith, first, in who you are, and second, in what you're doing. Belief involves *accepting* that a statement is true or that something exists. You can believe something without having a firsthand experience with it. For example, I can believe that jumping out of a perfectly good airplane with a parachute is terrifying. I don't have to experience it. You can believe things based on fact, observation, or the word of someone or something you trust.

Faith is a state of being. You can have faith with or without a religious affiliation to that faith. For instance, when you go to turn on a light switch, you have faith the lights will come on. When you get behind the wheel of your car, you have faith it will start. When you drive down the road obeying traffic signs, you have faith other drivers will do the same. Faith is putting hope and power into things we can't see now, but know we will see in the future.

I've learned that Emmanuel Teney, who is quoted at the beginning of this chapter, is right. When we have faith in something or someone, we no longer feel the need to control things. Things flow like they're going to flow, and we flow with them. It's one of the best feelings in the world to let go and let faith work. But faith doesn't stand alone. It requires belief. Faith and belief are what I call "The Power Twins" because I don't think you can have one without having the other. Neither of them, by the way, will work without you acting on them.

Belief without Action Is Dead

"In business, a nightmare is having a big dream and a bad team."

– John C. Maxwell

In his book *The Law of Buy-In*, John Maxwell asks, "Do you have a team you can trust?" He's not just asking about the team. He's asking about you. Can your team trust you? Do they believe that you believe in what you're selling? In other words, are you authentic? When we believe in something, we take action on that belief. That's faith. When I believe that my businesses are providing a good value and service to my clients, I do all I can to ensure that they continue to provide value. I hire great people. I train them well. I am honest in my transactions. I provide superior value for the money I charge. You need both head and heart to sell. You need experience, but you also need passion.

Sales isn't about talking to people and telling them facts and features about your product. It's about *believing* that what you have to offer your client is a solution to their problem. It's about believing that it can honestly help them. If you don't believe in the quality, the value, or the price of what you're offering, your customer or client won't either. You can't always use, or try out the things you sell, but when you can, do. There's nothing like first hand or hands-on experience with what you're selling to give you confidence in your product or service. This should go without saying, but you'd be surprised how many people sell products or services they have never used or know nothing about. Don't be that guy or gal.

If you sell large pieces of equipment or things you can't try or use, try to at least tour the factory where it's used. Talk with the people who do use the product on a daily basis. Find out what they like or don't like about it. The more you know your product or service and the people who use it, the better able you'll be to answer questions about it. Maybe you will never drive a large piece of industrial machinery, or wire or plumb some fixture, but you should understand it as if you have.

Know your industry. Understand what the common pain points and challenges are. This means listening to your existing as well as your potential customers. Depending on what you're selling, take a tour of different companies. Read the industry magazines. Follow people on social media.

Realize that as you begin the process of selling to your potential clients there will be failures. Don't attempt to look like you know everything. You don't. No one does. Be honest when you can't answer the questions your clients have. Tell them, "I don't know the answer to that, but I can find an expert who docs, and get back to you within 48 to 72 hours with an answer." Clients will appreciate that and won't think less of you for saying so. Be open to growing and learning something new about your product every day.

Don't pretend you understand something if you don't. Admit it. It's not a slam on you. When you're learning something, take lots of notes. You can't and won't remember it all, and you're bound to confuse things if you don't write them down and review them later. When you do fail (and you will), learn from the failure. Accept feedback, advice, suggestions, and even criticisms from those who know what's happening and who are trying to help. Don't be defensive. Do be humble. You don't have to take every suggestion offered, but you should accept it and sincerely thank the person for offering the insights.

Remember, you're building a relationship. Building a relationship means building trust. When people trust you the idea of doing business with someone else loses its appeal. Think about it, when you trust your doctor, or dentist, or mechanic, how open are you to finding another provider who wants your business? You're not. The energy, effort, and time it takes to find and build trust with someone else just isn't worth giving up what you have.

Get excited about what you sell. Believe in it at a cellular level. You can't do that if you don't engage with what you're selling. This is true whether you're selling tools at a hardware store, cars, lawn care, or catering. Know your product/service. See and experience it in action, and talk to those who use it on a daily basis. If you can't get behind it 100 percent, then maybe you shouldn't be selling it. If it's a great product, but not perfect in every way, but you still believe in it, then be honest about that when clients ask.

Clients want your honest opinion. If you can tell them the pros *and* the cons of a product, they'll respect that. Many of them are happy to work around the cons if they know what they are. You can't decide that for them, but you can and should be honest enough to give them that opportunity. What might seem like a con to you may actually be a plus for them. For instance, you may think it's important that a device or product has all the latest, greatest digital or electronic options—but your customer may actually see that as a con—because it means more service, more things to fail, and more upkeep for them. Don't assume because you don't see a feature as beneficial or helpful means your customer will feel the same way.

That's why you ask lots and lots of questions. Don't just ask questions to be asking them. Ask thought-provoking questions. Really seek to understand the issues your client faces. In doing the research for this book, I heard several stories from salespeople, including one of a woman who was looking for the "perfect" van. She just couldn't find the right van until a salesman asked her what she'd be using it for the most. She talked about carpooling for work, and travel. She talked about her daughter and son's soccer teams and how she was always having to make two trips to haul all the equipment, her kids, their friends, and her husband.

She was looking for a van that could carry kids and all the equipment, coolers, and supplies in one trip. But she didn't want such a large van that she would feel uncomfortable driving it outside of soccer season, or around town. In other words, she didn't want to drive a small bus or a huge van.

The solution the salesperson came up with was a rooftop carrier for the soccer equipment. That way the van would hold the children—and the equipment. And, it was a normal-sized van she felt comfortable driving outside of soccer season. By asking questions and putting himself in her shoes, he was able to sell her a car she loved, and that solved her transportation problem. Later, she told him the carrier was perfect for vacations and cross-country trips, even carpooling when people had bags that didn't fit under the seat. It seems like a simple and obvious solution, but sometimes buyers don't, or can't, see the obvious until you start asking questions.

At different times, all of us get too caught up in the problem to see a way out. It takes that outside person—you—to ask the right questions. As the expert on your product or service, you should know your product or service inside out so you can see the benefits of it for your customer. You're the problem solver. Buyers come to you for answers, insight, and your expert opinion. If you don't know what you're selling well enough to differentiate it from what everyone else is selling, then it's going to be difficult to convince your buyer why they should buy from you. If you can offer the product or service along with trust, service, and authenticity, then you've differentiated your company from everyone else.

Listen first, sell later. You don't know it all until your customer shares their concerns. They're going to value what's important to them, not you. You should do the same. What they value might be different than what you value. You might value the complex computer systems in a car, but someone who is a mechanic that works on their own car might hate them.

You don't know what someone needs, wants, or values until you listen, ask questions, find their need, and demonstrate you understand that need. Don't sell someone something just because they're looking to buy. Sell it because it's something that will make their lives, job, project, task, or work better. If you have experiences to share that are relevant, share them, but make sure the sharing relates to filling their need and isn't just a story to tell for the sake of telling. When you do this, your belief in what you're selling will create influence with your clients.

5

The Secret is W.O.R.K.

"You can't achieve a million-dollar dream on a minimum wage work ethic."

– Anonymous

The secret to successful selling is W.O.R.K. (being willing, being open, being real, and kicking it). So far, I've talked about a lot of concepts, faith, belief, knowing yourself, your personality, authenticity, and character. But what about sales techniques? Don't those matter too? They do.

For any technique to work, you have to establish a foundation, a culture, and an ecosystem where techniques *can* work. You have to be *Willing* to do the work on yourself, *Open* to changing the way you do things, *Real* with yourself about who you are and what you want, and you have to *Kick* those things into action once you understand the concept of *Selling from the Soul.* You can't just read this book (or any other), feel good, then put the book on a shelf and never take action on what you've read.

Now that you know what the foundation for *Selling from the Soul* is about (authenticity, being alive, and self-knowledge), let's move on to some actual selling skills and tips.

Qualify Your Buyers

The primary qualities most salespeople look for when selling to someone is: first, are they the decision maker in the sale, and second, can they afford it? That's great if you're looking for a one-time sale, but not if you're looking for a sustainable career.

When I qualify buyers, I want to know if they're the decision maker and if they can afford it, sure. But I also want to know if they're going to be a repeat buyer. Are they going to need this product or service again? Are they people with influence within their company? Are they going to be people I want to sell to over and over for the next however many years? Are they people I trust? Are they people I connect with? Do they have the *relationship potential* I'm looking for?

Build Value Around What You're Selling

Value can be hard to determine. Value has a lot to do with need and availability. The value of a bottle of ice water is greater on a hot day where no other drinks or liquids are available than it is at a location where there are free water fountains and other alternatives. Availability and scarcity contribute to value. The quality of the product contributes to value. Customer service and other options, such as warranties, guarantees, and money-back options contribute to value.

You'll have to determine what you can offer that adds value, or that explains the value, but you'll need to understand your customer's needs before you start talking about value. What you value might have nothing to do with what they value. Ask questions to find out what buyers value most:

- Customer service and 24/7 helplines

- Free replacements

- Image over price or vice versa

- Money-back guarantees

- Price over time

- Time over money

- Quality, and are willing to pay for it

- Long-term support

- An engaged, ongoing salesperson

- Upgrades

- Technology

- Choice—a range of color, styles, models, and features

But of all the things clients value, the number one thing that *all* clients value is *you*. When you put yourself into your buyer's shoes and can convey the buyer's pain points, and define their problem, then sales advance.

In a panel study with 530 B2B buyers, People First Productivity Solutions (PFPS) learned that buyers are more willing to meet with and more likely to buy from sellers who exhibit certain behaviors more frequently than others.[viii]

PFPS studies a range of behaviors, but some of their most fascinating results have to do with learning what buyers value. It's not what you'd think, but it's what I've learned over thirty-five years: buyers value relationships with sellers above all else.

Among the behaviors buyers value most are actions and attitudes that suggest the seller has a true ability to understand and empathize with the buyer. What PFPS also learned was that buyers thirty and younger place a higher value on seller behaviors related to building trust and connections. By contrast, B2B buyers over fifty valued seller behaviors related to driving return on investment (ROI) and business results. Universally, though, the top-ranked seller behaviors are those that demonstrate a seller's ability to engage and create an enjoyable connection and a relationship with the seller.[ix]

Like I've said over and over again, your buyers value most what you, their salesperson, can bring to the table. It's not your product. It's not your guarantees or price, or added bonuses. It's you. Buyers want the value only you can create. They crave the great customer experience only you can deliver. They want an enjoyable, beneficial experience that makes them feel good about their decision and their purchase. You're the only one who can give them relevant, timely, and useful information that will establish that connection. When you focus on selling behaviors, you neglect connecting behaviors.

So, stop focusing on positioning your product, start focusing on positioning yourself as a trustworthy resource. When you focus on closing the deal, you're losing sight of the need to open a relationship and clients pick up on that. It's an odd comparison, but clients like to be wooed and courted and to feel like they and their business matters. And it should. When you can create rapport through questions, listening, and educating your client, and making them feel good about your conversation, they will value the exchange.

Stay in an educational mode as long as you're influencing. When you influence others, you don't have to push for a sale or try to get them to buy. If you establish a relationship with your clients, they will walk down that path to purchase without any additional pushiness from you. As soon as you start pushing, you're going to break rapport and lose that sale. Rather than push towards a purchase, create a desire in your client for what you're selling. Do this through understanding their needs, putting yourself in their shoes, and honestly explaining the value of the product or service to them. Address their concerns. Answer their questions. Be patient. When they're comfortable with you and what you've had to say, then ask for the business and close the sale. And always ask for the business.

I learned this by accident. In the summer of 2003, a VP I knew and had done business with at her previous company invited me to their corporate headquarters to give a pitch for a large contract I really wanted. I showed up in shorts and a polo shirt, very casual attire, which was acceptable considering the place and the industry I was in. I had no formal pitch or fancy slides; it was just me and my confidence that my company could do the job they needed done. I assumed I was meeting the female executive I knew and had worked with in the past, but I would soon find out that wasn't the case.

There were other companies pitching for the job as well. Some were bigger. Maybe some were better. But they were competition. I entered the conference room in their top-floor office, and it looked like something you would see on Wall Street

— a full bar, pool table, and other amenities that look more like entertaining for a party than business. All the furnishings were first class, probably a quarter of a million dollars just in office decorations. The CEO and V.P. emerged for my presentation, which consisted only of my verbal proposal and my confidence. We talked and they were fine with my proposal, so I asked for the business right then.

The CEO didn't know what to do, and the V.P. just smiled. He then said he wanted to look over the proposals and think about it, but I persisted and asked again for the job. I did this three times. I left without a contract but got a call a couple of days afterward, awarding me the contract. The female VP, whom I'd worked with before, told me, "I don't have to tell you this, but I wanted you to know, you got the job because of all the companies who pitched us, you were the only one who asked for the business."

I wanted that job. That desire drove my boldness to ask for the business, but as a result, I learned something critical — always ask for the business. Let your buyer know you want the job. This goes for everything —whether you're interviewing for a job and you want the job, or if you're pitching a client. If you want the job, ask for it.

Don't Bad-Mouth the Competition

You're always going to have competition. Some will be better, some worse, some manipulative or unethical, some worthy of your respect, some not. Regardless of who they are, how they operate, their competence level—*never* put your competitors down. This is classless, and it shows your clients your immaturity. Instead, refocus the client's attention to the things you're providing and the service you're bringing.

Regardless of how strongly you want to put them down or disparage them, never talk bad about your competition. If your client brings up your competitors, acknowledge briefly what you know about their product or service in an objective manner, and then move on to what you're bringing to the table. Never focus on the competition. Focus on what you have to offer.

6

Confidence

"Inaction breeds doubt and fear. Action breeds confidence and courage. If you want to conquer fear, do not sit home and think about it. Go out and get busy."

— Dale Carnegie

Confidence is different from self-esteem. They may be related, but they're not the same thing. Confidence is the degree to which you believe that your actions will result in a positive outcome. When you're confident, you become competent. The more confident and competent you become, the more self-esteem you develop. You can't develop confidence without taking action—so, as Dale Carnegie says, don't sit home thinking about conquering fear, go out and get busy conquering it. There is never going to be a time when the stars align and all the conditions, including your fears and feelings about something, are going to be "right" for acting.

You can't wait or hope that they will. You have to just decide what you want and go for it. As you find your fears were misplaced, that you can do more than you imagined, that you're more capable than you thought, your confidence will grow. If you fail, you look at why you failed, make adjustments, and try again. That's life. It's how we all get through it. Those who embrace it and throw themselves into learning and trying again quickly rather than licking their wounds grow faster and more confident than the rest.

Confidence is something we develop with time and action. When people say they want more confidence they typically just need to take more action with the things they feel uncomfortable doing. Confidence can be had through repetition and practice and accomplishment.

Confidence is a belief in yourself. It's a belief and a knowing that whatever you promise someone, you will make it happen. Competence is developed by continual action and receiving feedback and learning and growing through your action. They work together to create success.

The Blueprint to Competence

Competence is developed through practice. More likely than not, you will fail. Everyone does one time or another. The difference between those who succeed and those who don't is that when they fail, they learn from their mistakes and keep going. That's where competence, and then confidence is born.

We all learned to eat, walk, read, speak, write, and do all the difficult things it takes to create a life for ourselves. At some point in our lives, we learned to work, manage money, pay our bills, drive, and hopefully how to interact with people. We do all these things to a greater or lesser degree of competence, but we do them. The better we do them (competence), the more confident we feel each time we do them.

Act as If

Some people call this the "fake it till you make it" solution. In a book that stresses authenticity, honesty, and transparency, encouraging you to "fake" something might seem disingenuous. It's not. When I say, "Fake it till you make it," I mean act "as if." I don't mean lie.

Acting "as if" doesn't mean being phony or inauthentic. Acting "as if" is about changing your behavior first and trusting that your feelings, competence, or confidence will follow. For example, when I started selling donuts to businesses, I didn't know the first thing about selling anything. I was uncomfortable, uncertain, and not sure what to say or do. I wasn't trying to impress anyone. I just wanted to sell donuts so I could eat. I was interested in changing myself, not in changing people's perceptions of me. My motivation was to sell donuts. So, I followed the lead of the people I was working with and acted "as if" I knew what I was doing.

Acting "as if" is a common prescription in psychotherapy. It's based on the idea that if you behave like the person you want to become, you'll eventually become that person. "Fake it till you make it" is great advice when confronting a personal situation in which you feel uncomfortable and must summon the strength you need to overcome it. However, when it comes to doing a job—a job people are paying money for and counting on you to deliver on—it's terrible advice. Here are some examples of acting "as if" from my own life:

- If you want to feel happier, do what happy people do—smile.

- If you want to get more work done, act productively.

- If you want to make more sales, do what successful salespeople do.

- If you want to be meet more people, introduce yourself to more people.

Acting "as if" means just that. When we wait until we think we're ready, we won't do anything. But research shows that changing your behavior first can change the way you think and feel. If you must get up in front of a group and give a talk and you're nervous and scared, act "as if" you weren't. Radiate confidence even if you're shaking on the inside.

When I partnered with my dad in our first business together, I knew how to work hard, and over the years I had learned how to sell. Most of our jobs were in the $700 to $800 range (remember, this was the 1980s). I went to bid on one of the largest jobs we'd ever had at the time—a $5,000 job. I talked to the guy, convinced him to let me bid on the job, and then I got a copy of the blueprint. I had no idea how to read it. I knew nothing about blueprints. I knew nothing about how to figure out what it would cost. I just knew I wanted this job. I acted "as if" I could do the job—not because I thought I personally could. But I knew that my dad had the skills the job demanded, and I knew we would get it done somehow. Later that day I reached out to one of the suppliers that we had, and the owner of that company helped me read the blueprint.

I put together a bid, made my pitch, and we got the job. I acted *confident*, and the *competence* followed. I was, and still am, continually developing me, my skills, and my knowledge of myself. You're always going to be running into new and different technologies, ideas, and products.

Experts now say that information is growing so rapidly that by the time someone completes a four-year college degree, what they've learned over the past four years is outdated and obsolete. So, you need to continually grow in whatever industry you're in. Confidence and competence come from stepping into the unknown. If you're confident, you hustle, and do whatever you can to provide excellence, people will buy what you sell because they like you, and they like your confidence. People don't buy products, services, or results. They buy you because you have made them feel good about their experience and time with you. It seems counterintuitive, but you need confidence before you need competence.

Trust me on this one. Your competence is only theory until there's enough action taken, and you have enough experience to know how things work. Then that confidence becomes competence. Confidence, in the beginning, will give you faith that your theory will work and the process you think will make these clients keep buying this product will give you enough oomph to get the sale. Once you make the sale, you become competent about how to deliver it.

I'm telling you, this is the way it works most of the time. Don't do this once and sit back and think that's all you have to do. You must keep refining and honing your skills. The more you develop you, the greater your confidence and competence.

The consistency factor is the other "C" I want to talk about. Confidence, competence, and consistency mean you keep growing you as you develop your selling influence. Look, I'm not for just having a bunch of confidence and hot air so people will buy something and then I say, "Oh, I'll figure out how to make it work later."

You ought to have a product, service or result that's already produced something and that you're excited about it. That's how you get trust and buy-in from your clients to start with. The reason people are buying from you is that they like you. They like your confidence, but they trust you can back up that confidence and deliver on your promises too. People buy from you because they like something you said, or the way you carried yourself, or how you came across in a meeting or pitch, or over lunch or a game of golf.

The point is this: it doesn't matter what you're selling. People don't buy products, services, or results. They buy you. Every time you step into a sales process with a client or a meeting where you've got multiple clients or however it is you do your sales—a phone call, a follow-up email—every time you do that, those people are not buying X, Y, Z or whatever it is that you're selling. They're buying you. They're trusting you.

This is why you need confidence first. They're trusting that you're going to do what you said you were going to do. If you don't over deliver and under promise, you're going to be in trouble anyway. Don't forget that one in this process.

But your competence comes after the confidence. Your competence comes by stepping into a place where you don't know what you're doing and then you gain the understanding as you do. Trust me. As your competence grows, so will your confidence. They build on each other.

The consistency of growing yourself, the consistency of you becoming better—more authentic, more skilled, stronger— follows. That first job that I sold where I couldn't even read a blueprint? I didn't know how to scale it, or even what a scale was. Well, in time, I learned how to read blueprints. I learned. I "grew me." That job was a one-page blueprint. Most of the blueprints we get now have ten or fifteen pages to them. Most of the blueprints I don't even read anymore. I could if I needed to. I developed that skill, but I have other people who do that now. Other things have changed as well. Most of that stuff is done through a computer or online where software does all the measuring and the counting. It's not even done by hand anymore. I used to freehand all this stuff, which took forever, but that's how I learned.

The point is that things change and you'd better grow and change too. If you don't continue to grow in whatever industry that you're in, it will change and leave you behind if you're not growing along with it.

When your industry changes, you better be making those changes. More importantly, you need to be seeing the changes that are coming. This is the reason for consistently growing yourself—through reading, learning, conferences, and classes. The confidence you got by selling that one-page blueprint won't be enough forever. You're going to need more competence and confidence to sell your company on completing a ten-pager. It's a lot more money, and people won't spend half a million dollars with you if they don't trust that you have the confidence for the half-million-dollar job.

Trust me. I remember when I sold my first quarter-million-dollar job. The first client that bought that much from me scared me. I didn't know how we were going to do it, but I had the confidence we could.

This job came along some eleven years after the company was started. I had some confidence, and I had a track record of competency. I had a reputation. I had delivered excellence to a lot of clients for over eleven years. But when I sold this job, it was so much bigger than anything we had ever sold to this client. He believed in us, but I was afraid that we couldn't do it. I bid the job, won the job, signed the contract, and we did the job and did it well.

After that, I started selling more jobs of that size and at that price. Why? Because I developed the competency through the confidence. I knew (belief and faith) that somehow we'd get it done, and we did. The client knew I'd done good work before and trusted me to do this job as well as I had others in the past. People aren't going to throw million-dollar jobs at you without history. You build that history as you build your confidence and competence—and show you're consistent.

What I want to leave you with is that if you're confident, you hustle, you get things done, and you make good on your words to your clients, you'll succeed. When you can't, for some reason outside of your control, deliver on your promises, you tell your clients why as soon as possible, and you eat crow, and you humble yourself. Clients will understand trustworthiness when you've made a mistake, or you over spoke, or something didn't come through the manufacturer, or another vendor didn't deliver in time. But whatever it is, your fault or not, own it. Be honest. Don't try to pull the smoke and mirrors trick over your clients. They'll know it. You'll be okay. You'll excel and surpass most people who do the same, just by owning your failures.

Your confidence is developed through action. Act "as if" and move forward even if you're feeling uncertain, scared, or inadequate. Competency comes through you getting yourself in a place where you're not sure if you can deliver all you've delivered.

Now, assuming that you've learned and studied your own product/service or whatever and you actually believe in it, you're doing better than 80 percent of the salespeople around you. You've got buy-in because you've used the product yourself and you've had a good experience with it. You know that it does what it's supposed to do, whatever that is, and you're excited about sharing it with others. You have a high level of buy-in at the core level. You become real and authentic in the way that you deliver your pitch to your clients.

You're developing your confidence by acting confident, and convincing clients that you already know what to do when you don't. You say, "That sounds backward." It does to most people. It doesn't to me. I'll give you some more examples from my own experiences. As I went into a business that had lots of potential, I would go to sell whatever particular thing we did—or thing we offered—and I had to price it. In learning how to price things, I had no clue where to start. I had no clue how to price work. I was twenty-three years old and hadn't been in this industry and had no idea what things cost. I would ask my suppliers and they'd give me prices they'd heard people were charging, but really I didn't know. I was incompetent. I developed competence by taking action.

In the beginning, I just went in and acted like I knew what I was doing. Think about this. I run a business. I talked them into giving me a shot at the job and I didn't even know how to read a blueprint. I want you to get this. This was my path for the first two or three years of this business. I wasn't competent in certain things, but I had confidence we'd get it done and we'd make money.

However, don't become so focused on confidence that you forget competence. When you get the work, figure out how to get it done.

There's a story told of how Bill Gates started Microsoft. He had developed the software but didn't have the operating system yet. He made an appointment with an investment banker that could take his idea to Wall Street and make him a multimillionaire overnight. Yet, when he called and made the appointment, he had everything but what you would call the piece that would make it actually work.

He didn't have that critical piece, but he set the appointment up anyway. Then he went to the person who created MS-DOS and bought it from him for $75,000. Think about this. He didn't even have the piece that would make his software work completely. He had it built, but he had to have the operating system for it to work. He bought MS-DOS, put it together, presented it, and the rest is history.

How do you do that? It's called having the confidence that you'll get it done. I think that most of the time we think that competency comes and then you'll develop confidence. This is what I'm trying to get you to understand through all of this. No, no, no. Develop confidence first, and competency will come. This is the way I've run my entire life. Most successful people will also tell you this is true. I'm not saying don't be competent in what you're selling or try to sell something you can't deliver on. I'm saying act, having the faith and confidence you can and will make it work.

That said, maybe you've heard of Frank Abagnale? He became one of the most famous con men ever. He claims to have assumed no fewer than eight identities, including an airline pilot, a physician, and a lawyer—all before he was twenty-one years old! And he was successful at each identity because of his confidence. He escaped from police custody twice (once from a taxiing airliner and once from a US federal penitentiary), also before he was twenty-one.[x]

Talk about confidence! Abagnale served less than five years in prison before starting to work for the federal government. He is currently a consultant and lecturer for the FBI academy and field offices. He also runs Abagnale & Associates, a financial fraud consultancy company.

Abagnale's life story inspired the Academy Award–nominated feature film *Catch Me If You Can* (2002). Abagnale's early cons included writing personal checks on his overdrawn bank account. This, however, would only work for a limited time before the bank demanded payment, so he opened accounts at different banks, eventually creating new identities to sustain this charade. Over time, he developed different ways to defraud banks. He would print out his own picture-perfect copies of payroll checks, deposit them, and then encourage banks to advance him cash based on his account balances. Abagnale would also magnetically print his account number on blank deposit slips and add those to the stack of real blank slips so when customers made deposits, the money was added to his account instead of the customer's account.

Later, Abagnale decided to impersonate a pilot to appear more legitimate when he was cashing checks. He obtained a uniform by calling Pan American World Airways (Pan Am) and saying that he was a Pan American pilot who lost his uniform while having it cleaned at his hotel. He was able to get a new uniform and a fake employee ID. He then forged a Federal Aviation Administration pilot's license.

Pan Am estimates that between the ages of sixteen and eighteen, Abagnale flew more than one million miles on more than 250 flights and flew to twenty-six countries by deadheading (flying for free as a pilot). As a company pilot, he was also able to stay at hotels free during this time. Everything from food to lodging was billed to the airline. However, Abagnale never flew on Pan Am planes, because he believed actual Pan Am pilots might spot him as a fraud.

I'm not encouraging you to do any of that. I'm using Abagnale as an example of what a teenage boy with confidence (and not much of a conscience) was able to accomplish by "acting as if."

Most people in business ask me for strategies. How do I get strategies and business plans? I'm like, "Dude, they're overrated." You're like, "Really?" I've built two multi-million-dollar businesses. In 2017, one of them was in the top one to two percent of companies in the United States in our industry.

Let me tell you what my business plan has been: go out, find more clients, sell more at higher margins, develop more revenue, and repeat the process.

I will tell you that we've developed process plans. We've developed processes, procedures, and plans. We've developed HR, we've developed strategies, we've developed hiring processes. We've developed a lot of things over time as we needed them. *But we didn't start with them.* We started with confidence and a simple plan: "Sell to more clients and create more revenue."

People ask, "Don't you want to start with all that in place?" Well, if the company is big enough and you have enough money to start with it all in place, yes, it's a good idea. But we didn't have a big company or a lot of money. We didn't have anything. We started with nothing. If you start as a Fortune 500 company and you go public and you have millions of dollars, then yes, you probably should have all the processes and procedures in place first. But most entrepreneurs *don't* start there. They start having nothing or very little other than buy-in and the excitement and belief and faith that they have a great idea and can build something. If that's where you're starting, you don't need a big elaborate plan.

You don't sell unless you have confidence in your product or service and you have buy-in in your product. You consistently grow yourself through self-knowledge, awareness, and learning. The more you know yourself, your skills, limits, strengths, and personality the more confidence you'll have when it's time to act "as if."

7

Excellence and Experience

"It's through repetition that possibility becomes ability."

— Anonymous

I learned a long time ago that I can talk. Believe it or not, I didn't know I had a gift for talking. But I had a wise mentor in my life in the 1980s.

After going through four years of having to sell or not eat, I was ready, eager, and hungry to learn how to sell. You know, it doesn't matter if you think you can sell or not if you're hungry enough. If you don't eat, you'll learn to sell. That was my option — sell or don't eat. I had a new wife who liked to eat as much as I did, only she didn't necessarily like having to eat at my grandmother's house every night. We lived on a farm right across from my grandmother. So, when we first got married, we visited my grandmother a lot, usually because she would have something going on in the food realm.

That was fine for a while, but we didn't want to wear out our welcome, and I didn't want to be poor or hungry forever. So, I learned to sell out of desperation. My first goal was to have more money than month. I started believing that this could happen.

But I had to go out and hustle and do my part to make it happen. It was about four or five years of hustling before I met the gentleman who became a mentor to me.

I was still afraid of standing in front of people and selling and talking, but I did it. I did a lot of it. That didn't mean I liked it. I did it against my natural fears and I got decent at it. But I didn't realize I had a gift for it until I was pushed into an experience I thought would destroy me—talking to a crowd.

I remember it like it was yesterday. It was December 31, 1988. This gentleman asked me if I would talk for five minutes in front of this crowd. He handed me a mic, and I had never spoke into a microphone before. I was scared. I said, "Man, five minutes. How am I going to talk for five minutes?"

People who know me today find that hard to believe. Now I tell people that I can't even say hello in five minutes. If you only give me five minutes to talk, you might as well not give me any time to talk. I can shorten subjects if I need to, but I like to have enough time to develop a subject.

So, this man put the mic in my hand and gave me five minutes to talk. It was like something came over me and changed me. I realize now that it was the presence of the Creator, who is my Father, that came over me. He said, "Son, you're going to do more of this." It was one of the best, unique, overwhelming experiences that I've ever felt. I did really well, and five minutes went by like it was five seconds. I felt like I hadn't said a quarter of what I wanted to say. But I ended my time because that was the requirement. It was an awesome experience.

The point is, you need to find your gifts and talents. You might be surprised, as I was, to find out you have a certain gift or a talent you just took for granted. Your gifts, talents, and abilities, at some level, are monetizable because the creator put them in you to create wealth at one level. Because you have to create wealth—or make money—to support your spouse and your family, or yourself if you're single. You need to create wealth to grow into the dreams and destiny you already have in your DNA.

Once you find those gifts and talents, you're on your way to creating that authentic voice about what you're selling. Some people say you have an authentic voice when you truly love a product and share that love. "Man, I bought that product. I love that product." Maybe it's an iPhone. Let's just use that. "I love the iPhone." It's real because you really do love the phone. But that's only one kind of authenticity.

What you have to learn is that out of the authentic voice you carry because you have experience with a product is how to influence others to buy that product. Your experience has got to come from a core level inside of you so that it's not just coming as head knowledge, but so it comes as heart and head knowledge. You have the head knowledge and the facts to back up what you're selling. But you also have the heart in it because you believe in it. You're not just feeling it, you're evangelical about it—you feel driven to convert people to this solution because you honestly believe it's the best answer to their needs.

Whatever product it is that you have chosen, you need to experience it at a deeper level. It's got to become part of you. People know when you're just pushing the product because it's popular, and when you're truly in love with it. There's an excitement about people who really love the product they're selling. Talk to someone who stands in line for twenty hours to buy a new iPhone and then to someone who waits until they go on sale at Walmart. You'll see and feel the difference in their voice and in their passion for the iPhone.

So, you have to:

- Develop your authentic voice.

- Believe in what you're selling at your core, not just mentally, but with your heart.

- Communicate that passion through your experience with the product, through your stories about it, and through how it changed you.

Now let's say you sell pharmaceuticals. Of course, you won't able to experience all the drugs you're selling, but you can deepen your knowledge of them by listening to the experiences patients have had and how their doctors feel and think about the drugs. If you can't talk to patients, talk to doctors. Talk to the people who write up the test studies. Read all you can about the different drugs you sell and the results people are getting.

I guarantee you the marketing department will love you. They spend a lot of time collecting stories, and they want their salespeople to use those stories and to be excited about them.

You need to understand the end user's experience and be able to convey that experience to others. Most of the time you'll be able to use the very products or services that you're attempting to influence others to buy. You can drive the car, cut your lawn with the lawn-mower, BBQ on the grill, or wear the cologne or perfume. When possible, use the products as much as you can. Remember any questions you had when you started using the product because your buyer is likely to have the same ones. If you're selling camping equipment, know how it fares in all kinds of weather, preferably from firsthand experience. If you don't use the product, know people who do and learn from their experience.

Pay attention to your own experience, good or bad, and have the four or five things that turn you on about it firmly in mind. Once you do that, you won't have a problem selling the product.

If you develop those three areas—an authentic voice, a core level belief in the product or service, and personal experience with the product—you'll sell well. Those three punches alone will make you a great influencer in selling whatever it is you're selling. I'll end there, and start the next segment with something amazing. What will you do with so great a freedom? Live free, my friend.

Build Excellence

One of the most critical things experiencing the product or service you're selling does is gives you experience. Out of experience comes feedback, and from feedback comes improvement, and over time improvement gives you excellence. So, excellence is built through:

- Thought

- Theory

- Action

- Results

- Feedback

- Improvement

- Excellence

It's a simple, logical loop, but you'd be surprised how many people fail to see where excellence comes from. You don't achieve excellence through repetition alone. You become excellent when you improve upon each repetition. When you're journaling, paying attention, looking for feedback, and learning from every experience, you grow. And as you grow, you improve. That's what growth is. Most people tend to see failure as a setback—but it's not if you realize that every failure has a silver lining, something that points to what you can do better next time.

There's always feedback in failure. It's that feedback that gives you the ability to have success down the road, if you know how to look for it. The problem is that too many people are so busy kicking themselves, or cursing themselves, or thinking about all they did wrong that they can't see the lesson in the experience. It's when you get something wrong that you learn how and where to get it right. You can take the right step at the wrong time, and face failure.

But it's that very experience, that failure, that ultimately builds excellence. That's why you must start tracking your progress now, today. That's why you journal. That's why you find a mentor. That's why you stop throwing pity parties for yourself. Answers come packaged as failures. The gift of failure is that it holds the secret to success. If you remember nothing else, remember this, "If you can't measure it, you can't manage it." Start tracking your failures. They'll teach you far more than your successes ever will.

8

The Structure Ecosystem

You can't manage what you can't measure."

— Peter Drucker

Strategy is a multilayered plan. I call this *The Trinity of Structure* which is Planning + Processes + Procedures = Major Profits. Let's start with an overview of how to create your own Trinity of Influence:

- Sell first, second, and third.

- Create systems around each thing you do and grow them over time.

- Don't let your plan stop you from doing your daily work of selling.

- Take an hour every day or every week (depending on the size of your company) and work on your business.

- Hire a trusted lawyer and an accountant as soon as possible.

- Develop a plan, policy, and procedure for every action you take to produce the best results.

- Measure your results continually.

The plans, policies, and procedures you develop at the beginning, whether you're a one-man army or a few people starting a big dream, will morph and change. Don't set these things in concrete and never revisit them. They need to be organic.

Well, okay there should probably be some things that you set in place in the beginning that maybe won't change. But I can tell you this: 80 percent of what you create should be pliable and organic so that as your business evolves, as you learn to work differently, as the economy changes, as your client base changes, as you change as a corporation and get larger, your plans, policies, and procedures will change too.

It's important to develop an ecosystem within your business and for the people you're hiring so that everyone in the company, not just the "salespeople," influences and sells. At our company, it doesn't matter what your job title is, you're still a salesperson. We do have levels of leadership now. We have Supervisor of Sites that are over three, four or five people. That's one crew.

Then we have Account Managers that manage from four to six different crews or supervisors. That means probably a hundred sites. Those are not always a hundred different clients. We have multiples sites with some of our clients. But that would be more of their job description.

Then we have a Vice President of Operations who is usually over a complete division. We're developing a Vice President of Sales and Marketing who will be over all the sales and marketing, the sales teams, and will teach our employees basically what I'm teaching you.

Then we have a Vice President of Human Resources and Management who manages all the HR responsibilities including payroll, clerical work, documentation tracking, hiring, job descriptions, hiring and firing policies, and more.

That's our company structure. Larger companies have many more VPs depending on what they do. I'm not going to go into that because each company's structure is different. I'm just trying to give you an overview of what we've built and are building in our company. That's why I said to keep the plans, policies, and procedures flexible and organic because we've adjusted ours and rewritten them as needed. Our job descriptions which were originally written in 2006 have been rewritten or adjusted over the years.

I will say that if you start hiring very talented people who are more skilled than you at some things, you need to develop a non-compete agreement. We have those, and every person from the Account Manager level or higher signs one when they're hired.

I would highly recommend that you draft one, have a lawyer review it, and put it in place when you start hiring talented, upper-level personnel. You hired them because they're smart and talented, and they could become a VP of your organization, another company, or their own operation. A non-compete will help protect what you've built.

Developing an ecosystem is part of developing your structure. I grew up in sales, and I'm the CEO and coach of the company. I talk to everyone. I talk to them about influence. I talk to them about how they talk to the managers when they're on-site with the supervisors. I talk to the account managers and I continuously remind people in our company that everyone sells. Everyone has influence, so call on it.

Your influence might be how well you communicate with your employees or your coworkers. You may have influence because you don't just ask them about issues they have on their individual site—you ask and then you solve the problem. When a supervisor answers a question that helps an on-site employee do their job and make a client happy, that's influence.

What I want you to get is that when you start developing a sales process of influence in your company, it should be everywhere. I don't care whether it's the VP of HR, or the person who stays in the office and estimates, they have influence.

If you have a staff member who has nothing to do with sales, but who answers the phone with a customer service attitude, they have influence. Employees don't have to go out in hand-to-hand combat in direct sales to make an impact. A friendly, helpful person who can answer questions, or promise to find someone with answers, can make or break a sale. At my company, everyone has influence. The same should be true of yours.

In our particular business, there are a lot of companies who don't know their cost of doing business. They don't know their overhead or their hourly rate. That's how we operated at first, too. Over the first twenty-two years we were in business, I learned intuitively how to price work. I knew some of our industry standards because I listened, and I talked to other people and tried to learn what they were doing.

I learned by listening, then by readjusting. You will find out how competitive you are when you bid for jobs against other companies. Sometimes you win and sometimes you lose. If you lose, typically, you will be told how far off your bid was from the winning bid. Then you start realizing, "Okay, this is how they price that. This is how they price this." If you're not listening and not learning, growing and changing, your experience is never going to change either.

My point is that I learned over the years how to do this, and how to do it really well because we stayed in business that long and we made money. There were probably three or four out of the twenty-two years that we had some losses on, but for the majority of those years, we hit them out of the park.

In 2006, I hired someone to do a structural assessment of our company. I said, "Tell me how to figure this up scientifically." He created elaborated and detailed job descriptions. We had descriptions to replace what we had. He helped with a lot of our HR needs, and developed an employee manual. I paid $60,000 to this consultant to put all this stuff in place. It might not sound like a lot of money if you run a large corporation, but it was a lot of money for me. I didn't even tell my partner at the time what we were spending because he wouldn't have liked it. But I did it, and it paid off.

To this day—we're twelve years removed from that—I can tell you exactly what our rate is. It doesn't matter if you have a business or if you're a one-man shop, I can get on the phone with you right now and give you a plan. All you need to do is tell me how much money you need to make a year and how many sales that you think you need to turn over a year to make that amount. I can tell you how many hours you'll work, and I can tell you how much money per hour you should make if you're just one person. If you're a member of team—large or small—I can give you a spreadsheet to systematically figure it out yourself. It's simple. It's a lot simpler than I thought.

It's interesting that over a decade plus two years, given our hourly rate, the only thing that fluctuates is our overhead. We're in a growth spurt, so our overhead has increased the last couple years, but by and large, our rate hasn't changed more than one to two dollars per person over the past twelve years.

It fluctuates up and down based on the economy and how much work we have. If we have a lot of work, we need to hire more people to get the work done. Sometimes when you're expanding, you make a little less margin at the top end. You'll understand that as you get into a business. The point is that I can tag it. I can tell you the high end and the low end of it twelve years later. I don't even have to open the spreadsheet.

You may not start out with systems, but you must develop them if you're going to build a large company. This is called an ecosystem of influence. No matter how many systems you have in place, don't forget the main thing, which is sales. If you don't sell something, you have nowhere to send people to go to work.

Sales are the motor that starts everything in your company. The critical aspect of having an ecosystem built around influence cannot be understated. If you understate it, you've missed the point. I don't care where you are on the DiSC profile. If you're an S or a C and you're not comfortable with sales, the best thing you can do is figure out how to grow the company fast enough to cover your income and raise enough money to create another job and hire a good salesperson.

If you hire someone and you don't learn any of the things I've just told you, you won't be able to sustain your business. If you don't have any implementation strategies and at least document these things so you know what you're looking for, you won't know how to measure the salesperson. This is why I'm giving you this stuff. These are all practical things, from the core level of belief in your product or service, all the way up to building an ecosystem that you can document on paper.

If you can review and learn from the things I'm sharing with you, listen to them, write them down, and then figure out how you want to implement them, you can develop your own manual. That manual will detail how to measure and how to hire a salesperson. If you have that manual, you'll have the specifications, the numbers, and the criteria to determine whether you hired the right person.

I've already told you that most salespeople are only going to close 20 to 25 percent of their sales. You know how many clients are walking in the door. If you have ten walking in the door every month and need to close five, you don't have enough people coming through your doors. You need twenty or thirty people coming in if you hope to hit that 20 to 25 percent. Figure out how to market well enough to get twenty or thirty people in front of your product so that you can have your salespeople—or salesperson, in the beginning—have enough leads to go after.

Your ecosystem is about documenting and developing a process of you moving into it, but it doesn't always have to be. I'm a D on the DiSC profile, so I just go out there and hustle my butt off. I don't have to worry about measuring me, because I do go out and hustle.

If you're a D too, you probably won't have to worry about measuring you. But in the beginning, if you don't take an hour each week when it's just you to measure your efforts and create a baseline, you won't know what to expect from an employee. You won't know if they're missing, hitting, or exceeding what you need them to do. That's the point of working on the business. You need to know what's possible, and what is not.

I love what John Maxwell says, "When you hire someone, if you can get them to do 80 percent of what you were doing in that particular task, give them the job, promote them and fire yourself. You move up. You do something different." Basically, he says you just worked yourself out of a job, and I believe that.

Don't think that anyone you hire is going to do 100 percent of what you do. They won't. I told you earlier that I closed almost 40 percent of my sales. I've never had anybody close anything near that amount unless we had an anomaly year. We've had a couple of years where the economy was so good that the supply and demand ratio was off, and businesses couldn't find people to do work. In those years, your salespeople will probably close more.

But if you take an average number of closings over time and measure it, 25 percent is a good number in our industry. Now, your industry might be different. It could be higher; it could be lower. You have to figure that out going out of the gate. My point is if you can get someone to do 80 percent of what you do, and they do it really well, give them the job, and find something else that you can develop.

You don't need to have an elaborate system. In the beginning, I had nothing. But it was only me. It might be only you right now. What I want you to understand is that if you want it to be more than you—and even if you decide that it's just going to be you—you still need to document what you're doing. That documentation doesn't have to gather dust in your filing cabinet either.

Create a curriculum that you can sell online that would help other people. All the things I've learned, the processes I've developed, and the wisdom I've accumulated are now available online for people to buy. I've learned a lot over thirty-five years. What I have to share is more than three and a half decades of learning and implementing and failing miserably and succeeding wonderfully. My documentation paid off early on, and now it's paying off again.

Regardless of how you're building your system, start building it around you today, and document everything you do. Create a curriculum for yourself and your employees. If you're like me, it may be a bit haphazard. If you're a C, like my friend Stephen, you'll have it lined up in wonderful detail as you go. Or, if you're an I, you'll be lucky if you ever write anything down. If you're an S, you'll probably be more like a C as far as documenting and organization.

The point is to do it the way you do it in whatever style you are, but do it. I talk better than I write, so most of the things that I document, I record on a voice memo and I get someone else to transcribe it and create a document. Do it the way you do it. If you're an I and are reading or listening to this, chances are you hate to sit down and do things because you're just so busy. I get it. You're moving all the time. You won't have time to write it all down. So, get a portable mic. I use one from Motiv called Shure. It connects right to your iPhone. There are a couple of models, but get the nice one that looks like one you can sing in it.

When you have a thought or find something that works, take the time to document it. If you can't sit still long enough to type it out, document it through a voice memo. Then you can go back later, listen to yourself, and write it down or have an assistant or a transcription company transcribe it for you. Save it so you'll be able to document it.

This is how you begin to build a system that other people can fit into when they join. It will be more seamless, and you'll be more successful than you thought you could be if you do this when you're small.

9

The Created Atmosphere

Nature, which is an ecosystem, includes all of the living things in a given area. It's the system in which those things interact with each other and with their nonliving environments (weather, earth, sun, soil, climate, atmosphere). Each organism has its own niche or role to play. In your world, company, or industry, other ecosystems exist whether by design or default, to your benefit or your detriment.

That's why it's important that you create the ecosystem you want to have, preferably one where *everyone* influences and *everyone* sells—and I mean *everyone*. Every employee—janitor, receptionist, human resources staff, vice presidents, presidents—*everyone* who works for you should be influencing and selling with their actions, body language, tone of voice, and customer service, even if they never give a sales pitch.

For instance, I have someone at my office who answers most of the phone calls when she's there. She's as nice as can be to everybody in the world. When people talk to her, they want to buy from our company. Period. Why? Because she sells them on doing business with us with her words, her attitude, her demeanor, her aliveness, and her passion for what we do.

I want you to get this at a core level, even if you think, "I just want to build something through the internet where I sell stuff." Let me tell you something, if you build something of any size, eventually, you're going to need an executive assistant, a secretarial staff, and maybe even a human resources staff.

Eventually, you might also want one or two other salespeople. Even if it becomes an entrepreneurial venture where you create the products to sell online, you might need marketing and you might not want to contract it out. You might find a marketing director, or you might be the marketing director.

In the beginning, you may think you can do everything yourself because the Internet will magically sell everything that you have. But you have to consider where you're going. Jeff Bezos, the founder of Amazon.com, started out boxing items in his family garage.

I don't know if he thought about an executive secretary, or about his system when he was running Amazon shipping from a bunch of folding tables set up in his driveway, but I'm going to guess he did. You can't run your business thinking it's never going to grow any larger than just you. Even if you'll always be a one- or two-person corporation, you must develop an ecosystem of influence in those one or two people.

Being a one-man band or company is fine. So is being a multimillion-dollar and multi-employee corporation. Whatever your dreams and destiny are is what it is. There's nothing wrong or right with either path. The more you develop an ecosystem of influence in each employee, the easier it is to develop the sales process and scale your company as you go.

We're going to get into some hand-to-hand combat and tactical things here. There are plans and procedures to follow, and things to document and measure as you go to determine if you're succeeding. The nuts and bolts are important, but it's critical to your ultimate success to understand how vital the mental and emotional game is. That whole *Selling from the Soul* connection, my urging you to influence your clients and potential clients with your passion and authenticity is real. It's foundational. If you're doing it right, you'll grow. You'll have to do it right if you want to take care of the business you're bringing in.

If you do grow a company to more than two people, add at least one salesperson to be influencing people too.

If you grow even larger, hire more salespeople. Still growing? Strongly consider adding a sales team. But don't just add salespeople to create a team. Pick salespeople whose gifts, talents, and abilities align with the qualities that make them the best person for your team, and your company. It sounds a lot simpler than it is, but you can do it. You must do it.

A business cannot succeed without sales. Whether you're selling a product or a service, your sales staff should be creating and sustaining relationships that ultimately sustain your business. That's not a task just any salesperson can do, so take your time and hire wisely. And make sure you're hiring people for *your* ecosystem! The only way to do this effectively is to write it down.

You can't change what you can't measure. You can't measure what you haven't documented.

Define Your Industry and Your Company Ecosystems

Until you have a foundation, including a good idea of who you are, what your goals, motivation, and passions are, you can't really begin to create the ecosystem I've described. Why? Because your ecosystem, your company culture, and your brand revolve around who you are. If you don't know who you are, or what's important, or what your mission is, it's difficult to create goals or systems of any kind.

You need to develop systems to build a larger company. It's impossible to grow a business if you don't who you are, what you want, what matters, and what makes you want to get up in the morning. It's like saying, "Get in the car, today we're driving!" You can drive all day, but you'll just burn up time, gas, and resources and have nothing to show for it if you don't have a destination.

Let's start with the basics. There are two ecosystems. One is your industry ecosystem, which is the network of organizations and people, including suppliers, distributors, clients, competitors, agencies, and so on, who are involved in the delivery of a specific product or service through both competition and cooperation. The other is your personal business ecosystem (the umbrella for your company's *cultural system* which I'll talk about later). In any ecosystem, efficiency is rewarded by survival. Inefficiency, on the other hand, is punished by extinction. That alone should motivate you to think about your ecosystem!

The idea I want to stress is that each person in every ecosystem affects and is affected by the others in that system. If you have employees in your business who aren't working according to that ecosystem, like fish in a desert or bears and wolves in a suburb, you need to help them find another system where they *can* thrive. Then you need to go back and attract the kind of people who will thrive in your ecosystem. Your business must always be creating a constantly-evolving relationship in which each person in it is flexible and adaptable in order to survive, just like in a biological ecosystem.[xi]

A lot of people confuse ecosystem with culture. Culture is what happens within an ecosystem. Culture is how people get things done inside a company. Culture includes written and unwritten rules, systems, procedures, ethics, standards, and so on. But it's the ecosystem itself that defines how that culture evolves and operates.

For instance, I think of our landscape management company as an ecosystem of influence. That means that everything we do, from answering the phone to delivering products and services, is about influence and selling and taking care of our clients. Our culture—how that influence gets done, or the form it takes—is defined by our ecosystem. Our managers, salespeople, and employees create the culture, which is how they do things to ensure our ecosystem of influence is maintained. Each of them has their own way of doing things, making decisions, using their gifts, talents, and personalities, but they all still operate under the umbrella of influence.

If our company's ecosystem was a greenhouse, for instance, our culture would be all the different kinds of plants living inside that greenhouse. The plants (people) would all be unique and have different seasons, different needs (water, nutrients, and so on), but they'd all be living and growing in a specific kind of greenhouse that provides the ecosystem for them to thrive in. If our ecosystem was for succulents (plants that don't need a lot of watering or high humidity), then plants that need daily watering and high humidity wouldn't do so well there because the culture in that ecosystem (greenhouse) would be low water and low humidity.

If you have a business ecosystem like we do, where influence and selling from the soul is how we're set up, then a culture where clients are ignored isn't going to happen, and if it tries to, it will fail. So, your culture arises from the ecosystem. If your CEO, CIO, and everyone from the president to the receptionist is operating in a system where influence, heart, passion, authenticity, and self-awareness is what drives the company, your culture is going to evolve into actions, systems, and practices that mirror those values. Anything or anyone that doesn't fit into our ecosystem—like selfishness, lack of follow-through, apathy for the product or service—isn't going to survive here.

Ecosystems are dynamic. That means they're constantly recreating themselves, and reacting to disturbances and events happening around them (fire, tornados, flooding, drought, etc.) and to the competition among and between the things that live in that system.

Think about Yellowstone National Park. Maybe you heard about how things changed when wolves were reintroduced. You wouldn't think something like a few dozen wolves would have an immense impact on the entire ecosystem, but it did. The handful of wolves that were introduced into the park actually began to not only change the shape and flow of the rivers inside the park, but they altered the entire ecosystem—from beetles and bugs to birds and other wildlife—in a very positive way.

How? First, the introduction of a few wolves into the park changed the behavior of the elk population. The wolves, who feed on elk, forced the elk to stop being fat and lazy and standing in one place all the time, browsing on all the willow trees. That browsing was stunting the trees' growth. That stunted growth kept the tree population down, which in turn kept the beaver population down, because beavers also fed on the trees.

With predators in the park, the elk had to stay on the move. Since the elk were no longer standing around all day browsing on willow stands, the willows had a chance to grow and thrive. With fewer elk eating up their food of choice, the beavers had greater access to their natural food: the willow trees. As the trees grew, their population recovered and produced more food. The increase in willow stands attracted the beavers, who cut down the trees and built more beaver dams. The increase in dams altered the flow of the rivers.

But that's not all that happened. Beavers also change how water is stored, so they not only recharged the water table, but their dams and ponds provided cold, shaded water for fish. So, the fish population grew. The now healthy willow stands also provided habitat for songbirds. Not all those fat elk were able to escape the wolves. The carcasses the wolves left from their kills attracted bugs and fed predator birds. Everything in the park was impacted in some way. All those changes, even the most minute, came from introducing one thing—wolves—into the ecosystem. I've oversimplified the process, but you can read the full story online.[xii]

You don't know what things will or what can happen when you introduce something or someone, no matter how small or large, into an ecosystem. That's why you have a variety of personalities and people (DiSC) to ensure that at least part of them can cope with any new situation; and you have a culture in place to ensure that while the ecosystem may evolve or change, it's still essentially the same ecosystem. Yellowstone is still a forested park (ecosystem), but things improved when a new thing was introduced. You may already have an *ecosystem of sales*, but what happens when you introduce selling from the soul into it? How will it change?

Create Your Ecosystem

How do you start creating your ecosystem? Remember that journal I keep referring to? Start there. Document what you do and why you do it. Document if it's working or not. You can't measure or evaluate something for which you don't have a baseline. Track your failures as well as your successes to accurately measure what's working. By writing down your strengths, values, policies, and goals as you go and grow, you're creating the ecosystem you want to live and work in.

Start building your ecosystem around you. Create a curriculum around what you do. Teach, train, and reinforce this to your employees at all levels. Whatever system you create can be used in future additions to your team. Cover your weaknesses with other people's strengths. Build a system that other people can fit into.

10

Rapport

"You can make more friends in two months by becoming interested in other people than you can in two years by trying to get other people interested in you."

— Dale Carnegie

We all know people who seem to be able to strike up a friendship, a connection, a rapport with people the minute they meet them. It's just a gift—something we mere mortals can't achieve. Or can we? We can. And if you want to be a successful salesperson, you'll learn and practice this skill every chance you get! Don't worry. No matter your personality type, you can learn to establish rapport.

As a father of two girls, I initially thought "girls were girls," and that I could interact with them both the same way. I was wrong. I quickly learned that if I wanted to build rapport with my daughters, I had to understand them individually. They were different personalities. To engage effectively with them, I had to learn how they thought, and how they wanted me to interact with them. My oldest daughter was like most firstborn children. She wanted to do things herself, her way. I learned that she wanted to understand something fully to get more information and then attempt to do it herself, her way.

My younger daughter would normally just go and do things without wanting any input from me in the beginning. When she was only three and a half years of age, she decided she was going to swim without any flotation aids. On the very same day she also jumped off a diving board into nine feet of water! She never had swimming lessons. She took off the flotation devices and dog paddled to the side, and then jumped into the water again! All of this without my input other than making sure she didn't sink.

I had to establish rapport with each of them based on how they preferred to engage. You can do the same with your clients, family, friends, and even strangers—once you understand your personality type, and theirs. This is why I stress the DiSC Personality Profile. It helps you understand the differences among people.

Everybody is different. You don't sell to a doctor the same way you sell to an engineer. You don't sell to a housewife, accountant, or small business owner the way you sell to a consultant.

My friend, Stephen, worked at a large pharmaceutical company for twenty-five years before launching his consulting business. He's a great salesperson because he's led marketing teams all over the globe. He helped his company roll out products that were north of $100 million in value if they were sold correctly.

Stephen worked for a large company with about 100,000 employees and had a lot of experience before going into business for himself. However, if I were to interview Stephen for a position as a salesman for my company, I probably wouldn't pick him if I only looked at his DiSC profile (he's primarily a C). His personality profile alone doesn't tell me what a great and successful salesperson he really is. Remember, he sold pharmaceuticals to doctors who likely were very analytical, critical thought process type people, which would fall mainly into the C style in the DiSC. He was a perfect fit for a pharmaceutical sales job!

So, while personality tests can be helpful, they're not perfect. Use them as guidelines, but don't base your final decision on a score or a profile. Great salesmanship depends on who you're selling to and what you're selling.

I developed a life metaphor a long time ago: "Everybody sells." If you're reading this and saying, "Well I don't sell," did you get married? If you got married and you're a guy, you probably sold yourself to your mate in some way, shape or form even if you had to promise her the world to do so. If you're a woman and you're married to your husband, you used your influence, skills, and personality to influence him when he started liking you and you liked him back. You both "sold" yourselves to each other. You used different means and approaches, but essentially you followed the same sales process talked about in this book.

Instead of looking at persuading people as "sales" because the term *sales* seems to have such a bad name, let's look at selling for what it really is—influencing someone to buy or buy into something. When I influence people because I've had a good experience with a company, do they buy products from that company if they're my friends and trust me? Yes, if they have that need. That's why so many companies want to find and work with influencers. They know how much power a good influencer can exert. Word of mouth is immensely powerful, but word of mouth from a proven influencer is golden. It practically ensures sales.

For instance, if I buy a car and I had a good experience at a car dealership, I'm going to recommend that dealership to any friend I have who is looking for a similar make and model. If I bought a Ford truck at that dealership, then they would probably go see the person that I dealt with and speak with them first. If they were treated as honestly and professionally as I was, they would probably buy their truck from the same person, and the same dealership.

Now, if my friend has a good experience and he recommends the same dealer, and mentions I got a good deal too, the influence we have together helps boost that dealership's sales without them having to do anything other than live up to the good experience they've already delivered. On the other hand, if that dealership got greedy and started taking advantage of the people their first good reports attracted, it won't be long before they destroy their reputation and the influence they had created in the first place. What influence really means is "caring." I also care for my clients. I want their best, even if I don't benefit from my interactions with them.

Clients may need a service I don't provide. Instead of attempting to provide a service when I can't, I refer them to someone who can do the best job for them in that area. That's how I build my influence. My clients know I'm going to do the best job I possibly can do for them and they will receive the best treatment from myself and my employees. They don't have to worry about how I'm going to deal with them because they trust me. I have influence with them.

The important thing here is to stop looking at sales like you're selling commodities whether you're selling door-to-door or selling face-to-face. The most critical aspect of selling in today's world is developing personal relationships with your clients. Even over the internet, selling is really about building for the long term, not just one sale and you're done. In fact, this is especially true online. So, the way I want you to see yourself is as a person who can be trusted and only influences when it's a win for both you and your client. I call this "being a selling influence." Everyone sells, they just do it better or worse based on how they are able to influence others to buy.

I'm mentoring people right now who I wouldn't hire at my company for sales because I don't think that they would enjoy the way we sell. The way we sell is different. Because I grew up in the typical type sales environment, I actually did sell door-to-door and I did sell a commodity. I love sales, I love teaching it, and I love helping people who are in sales who have the ability to step into it more, and in a way that shows they grasp being a selling influencer and understand people's different styles. What are those styles?

People who have both **outgoing** and **people-oriented** traits often exhibit *inspiring* and *interactive* behaviors. They usually focus on interacting with people, having fun, and/or creating excitement.

People who have both **reserved** and **people-oriented** traits often exhibit *supportive* and *steady* behaviors. They usually focus on preserving relationships and on creating or maintaining peace and harmony.

People who have both **reserved** and **task-oriented** traits often exhibit cautious and careful behaviors. They usually focus on facts, rules, and correctness.

Some styles, like the DI, or ID style, are drawn to sales in greater numbers, but all styles can sell. People ask me, "Hey, how do I find clients and how do I sell if I'm not a salesman, or a DI, or an ID style personality?" That's a great question. I've got a salesperson working for me who is a CD-style and she's doing a great job because she's selling to people who are mostly Ds. There's a relatability factor and a gender factor there. Don't let your style stop you. Learn to use your style's strengths.

I tell all people, "Use what God gave you." The Creator made you a certain way and He expects you to use every bit of that because those things are all part of your gifts, talents, and ability. Even your outward person, the way you're built, the way you look are gifts. It could be the color of your skin or your gender—those are part of your gifts. Some of us are athletic, others are not. We all vary in looks, size, weight, and physical attributes. But whatever those attributes are, it's the heart and soul that come through the strongest. You may attract people to you because of your age, looks, or physical attributes, but people stick around based on the heart and soul they find.

When I talk about your selling, I'm not talking about manipulating people with your talk and actions. I'm talking about being the authentic you and influencing them. If you've heard any of my talks, you know I don't believe in causing people to buy for the wrong reasons in any way, shape or form or influencing them that way. I believe in influencing others from a state of excellence, authenticity, and vulnerability. I think you should sell because what you have, what you believe in, and what you have to give are the result of a great product or service. You're selling because you can offer a great experience to your client. They want to buy from you because they see that you're going to provide excellence, both in the product and the service you deliver. They trust that you're going to deliver not only what they are looking for, but above and beyond what they're looking for. That's what I believe sales is about for people.

I don't believe in taking advantage of people. I believe that the Creator, my spiritual father, set up the universe to be an advantage to givers. If you sow enough, you'll reap so much that the reward will come back on every wave. You ask me, "How do you know that?" Look at any tree. The Creator made all the trees. If you look at a fruit tree or if you look at seasonal vegetables, what do you see? Look at a cornstalk. If you put one seed in the ground, how many ears of corn do you get? If you plant one apple tree, how many apples to do you get off that tree in a lifetime?

Drive up the coast or anywhere in Northern California. Ride north on Highway 5 and you'll see all kinds of farms for miles. You'll see almond trees and olive trees. If you plant one olive tree, how many olives do you get off that tree in a lifetime? The most amazing thing to me is that you get all that from only one seed. It's the same with people.

The world operates on the adage that we will reap what we sow. What I want you to understand about sales is that there are prototypical sales people if you grow a company where you need "salespeople." I keep coming back to Stephen as an example because I've known him for years now. He has great integrity and is excellent at what he does. He's a hardworking person. His work ethic is golden. When he was working at his last company, he was working two people's jobs and still producing at a high level. But he sold mainly to people who were doctors, people who thought as he did.

Think about that. I imagine his sales were a lot like selling to an engineering firm where people are Cs and they think about things in detail and prefer accuracy. He's naturally like that so he clicked with them. He could sell skateboards to extreme skaters, but it would mean adapting his personality style to theirs. Sales success really depends on the industry that you're in and how it matches up with your personality. That's one thing that I want to get to you. If you're a C and trying to sell to clients who are mostly I's, you might want to consider finding a company whose clients are more in line with who you are. Or get very, very good at understanding the other letters in the DiSC that you don't naturally relate to. Remember people want you to communicate with them, based on their personality style, not yours.

This is the other spot I want to hit. If you haven't listened to my other talks, I have four or five on the DiSC profile and some variations that I've built around it. My mentors have given me advice over the years that I think will help you easily understand it. You can simply take the test, and read the books as well. I started by taking the DiSC test itself. It completely changed my approach to sales. Here's some of what I've learned:

If you're selling to engineers, you want to be a high I. Unless that I has a D, typically they don't drop in the S, but you'd rather have a DI, DC, or CD if you're selling to engineers. As I said, it depends on who your client is. Although there are prototypical salespeople for certain things and for most things, there are some niche industries.

Stephen's company was still dealing with physicians. He has a Ph.D. as well. He's a doctor of pharmacy. He understood from a scientific side how the drugs he sold worked in people's bodies and could explain that to the doctors who prescribed them.

He has a lot of knowledge the average pharmaceutical salesperson might not have. Knowledge and experience will often overcome any sales inadequacy you have. People will buy from you because you know your product or service, and they like, trust and respect your credentials as much or more than they like you. However, I'm here to tell you, if you bring your clients excellence and you bring them a finished product that exceeds their expectation and you under promise and over deliver consistently, I don't care which one of the letters you are on the DiSC profile, they'll keep buying from you. Period.

The DiSC and the Internet

So much of the world today is built around online marketing. It's getting harder to market and to be seen. But the internet will continue to connect us. People worried that digital devices would isolate us from relationships, but they've done the opposite. We have conversations and relationships online that we might not have the time or energy for in person. We desire deeper face-to-face relationships with people we know online, especially introverts. I'm telling you the internet has not isolated society; it's made society bigger. It's also become a tool, if used correctly, to help you build your business.

I've seen how selling has changed. I've sold for three and a half decades. I've sold everything! But I started somewhere too. I wasn't always able to sell. When I was nineteen, I did two things that changed my life forever. I met a gentleman who would become my mentor, and I started hanging out with a group of people I really enjoyed. A couple of the guys in this group were really sharp. They were sales-people. They could talk people into buying things.

I didn't know anything about sales. I'd never thought about it. However, I was inspired by this particular gentleman and eventually, I followed him around in business. He mentored me, and he helped me grow for about four years. For the first year, he taught me the things that he knew. In the first few months, he taught me about sales, then he put me out on the side of a curb, literally, in a small town in the South close to Burlington, North Carolina, where I sold donuts door-to-door to businesses.

Think about this. Krispy Kreme donuts, if you're familiar with them, are pretty much loved anywhere in the world where people eat donuts. They almost sold themselves. I would sell boxes of Krispy Kreme donuts for $2.50 a box. I would also sell boxes of mixed donuts for $3.50 to $4.50 a box. I would sell from early in the morning until about lunchtime every day, which is when people want donuts. I sold these donuts door-to-door in four or five cities. I created my own routes; my mentor showed me how to do that as well. I was newly married and living in a very small apartment. For the first four years of our marriage, that's how we lived. We were poor. We had nothing. I had to find a way to make money, so we didn't have to eat donuts, or eat at my grandmother's house every night.

I would sell donuts, then I would rest some. At night, we would sell another product, which was a multilevel marketing thing. It was during the four years I sold donuts and multilevel marketing products that I learned how to talk to people and how to sell.

I also sold vacuum cleaner services and vacuum cleaners door-to-door in Greensboro, North Carolina. I sold alarm systems and education, and even classes on learning how to drive an eighteen-wheeler. Think about that. Selling people on attending a tractor-trailer driving school. I can't think of all the different things I've sold, but there were four, five, maybe six to eight different things I sold over four years. I learned either you sell, or you don't eat. I learned how to talk, and how to get people to buy. I'm not complaining. It was a great time, but it was a time of learning, growing, and discovering all the things I'm sharing with you so you don't have to do the same thing.

I got a great education from great salespeople who knew how to influence on many different levels. They were all great salespeople, and they were all at different places on the DiSC profile.

Well, this non-collegiate, four-year education in sales led me to a complete other industry. Those experiences led to where I ended up. I got the equivalent of a master's degree in four years of selling every kind of thing you can think of. And if I could tell you the one thing that made the biggest difference in my sales success it would be that people want you to communicate to them the way they want to be communicated with. I will give a few examples below of the four major types of people you will meet and their preferred method of communication.

The DiSC Profile

I keep referring to the DiSC Profile. What is that? It's a nonjudgmental tool used to help people understand their own personality and those of others. It explains people's behavioral differences, preferences, and communication preferences. There are no right or wrong answers to the test, and the test doesn't measure intelligence, mental health, or values.

DiSC profiles describe human behavior in various situations. For example, the DiSC questionnaire asks how you respond to challenges, how you influence others, how you respond to rules and procedures, and your preferred pace of activity. It doesn't measure every dimension of your personality but gives you a general overview of how you engage and prefer to communicate with your world and those around you.

We all have all four reference or "personality" points, but we prefer to use one or sometimes two points or styles. Someone can be primarily a D personality with a secondary personality of I, S, or C. While most sales-people are D's and I's, or a DI or ID combination, all profiles can be successful sellers if they understand how to build rapport and how to sell.

The DiSC model discusses four styles:

1. Dominance: direct, strong-willed, and forceful

2. Influence: sociable, talkative, and lively

3. Steadiness: gentle, accommodating, and soft-hearted

4. Conscientiousness: private, analytical, and logical

D Personality

I'm a D or dominant personality. I like to charge ahead and get things done and worry about the details later. Stephen is a C. He prefers to take his time and examine all the details and get things right the first go around.

D personalities tend to be fast-paced and outspoken. We question everything and have skeptical traits, but we also act assertively, make quick decisions, and speak rather bluntly. We're always looking for ways to maximize efficiencies and results. But we don't want to be given an easy win. We also love a challenge. Being in a relationship with us can be challenging. We struggle to show empathy. You might have to ask a D to show more patience.

If you're selling to us, give us the bottom line, be brief, focus your discussion, avoid making generalizations, don't repeat yourself, and focus on solutions rather than problems.

I know these things, and more, about myself. I know how I can come across to people. So, when I'm selling, unless I'm selling to another D personality, I listen and try to understand the personality of the person I'm engaging with.

I Personality

When I'm selling to or engaging with an I personality, I know they like to control their environment by influencing or persuading others to their point of view. When I'm communicating with an I personality, I know I need to share my experiences and allow them time to ask questions and to talk themselves. I know I need to focus on the positives, avoid overloading them with details, and not interrupt them.

A person with an I personality:

- Can be impulsive and disorganized and lack follow-through

- Is often very popular, because they're convincing, magnetic, enthusiastic, warm, trusting, and optimistic

- Prioritizes taking action and collaborating with others, and is enthusiastic about the projects, people, and things they're engaged with

- Is motivated by social recognition, group activities, and relationships

- May fear loss of influence, disapproval, and being ignored

- Values coaching and counseling, freedom of expression, and democratic relationships

- Values friendships and happiness

- Likes to have authority and values prestige status symbols

- Likes being popular

- May fail to follow through completely with tasks and projects

- May fail to research all the facts

- May fail to speak directly and candidly

- Struggles to stay focused for long periods of time

S Personality

Have you ever met someone who worked hard to make sure everyone got along, and wanted to keep the peace at all costs? You might have met an S-style person. People with an S personality prioritize cooperating with others within existing circumstances to carry out whatever project or task they've been given. They're the peacemakers in life. I know that when I'm selling to or engaging with an S personality I need to be personal and amiable. I need to express an interest in them and let them know what I expect from them. I can't just barge into their office or life with my demands though. I need to take time to provide clarification, to be polite, and to avoid being confrontational, overly aggressive, or rude—all ways a D personality can come across just by being a D!

A person with an S personality:

- Is motivated by cooperation

- Looks for opportunities to help others and solve problems

- Values sincere appreciation from others of their efforts to help

- Supports others; collaboration and maintaining stability make them happy

- Is often described as calm, patient, predictable, deliberate, stable, and consistent

- May be indecisive or overly accommodating

- Have a tendency to avoid and even fear change

- Fear a loss of stability

- Don't like offending others

- Value loyalty and security

- Value personal accomplishments and acceptance by the group or team

- Prefer to gain their power through formal roles and positions of authority

- Like the status quo and a controlled environment

- Don't adapt quickly to change or unclear expectations

- May find it difficult to multitask

- Don't like to promote themselves

- Don't like to confront others

C Personality

C personalities emphasize working conscientiously. They are detail-oriented people, and like to work within existing circumstances to ensure quality and accuracy. When I'm communicating or selling with a C personality, I know if I want to make a sale I need to slow down, focus on facts and details, and minimize the excitement or emotional language my D-style tends to use. And I've got to be patient, persistent, and diplomatic with them. My usual D-style will turn off a C-style. We're opposites on the DiSC chart.

But if I know that I can rein in my style and appreciate theirs. I can communicate with them in the way they prefer to be communicated with. I'm not manipulating—I'm accommodating.

A person with a C personality:

- Is motivated by opportunities to gain knowledge, show their expertise, and demonstrate they do quality work

- Prioritizes accuracy in what they do

- Likes to maintain stability

- Often challenges assumptions, preferring facts

- Often are described as careful, cautious, systematic, diplomatic, accurate, and tactful

- Can be overly critical

- Can be accused of "paralysis by analysis," as they tend to overanalyze and isolate themselves

- May fear criticism and being wrong

- Value quality and accuracy

- Like to achieve unique accomplishments

- Like to be right

- Like correctness and stability

- Prefer predictable accomplishments

- Pursue personal growth

- Can find it difficult to let go of things and to delegate tasks to others

- May find it difficult to compromise their need for accuracy or detail for the good of the team

- Can struggle to join in social events and celebrations

- Find it difficult to make quick decisions

These are very general traits of each of the DiSC personality styles. Your life experiences, education, background, age, and maturity levels can also influence your personality style. For instance, no two D's are the same, but they will share general personality traits. There are books about the DiSC, and even about how to sell to the different personality types. I include these descriptions here to give you an idea and overview of the DiSC. I strongly urge you to take the test and to learn about how you interact with others based on your unique profile.

Remember, the DiSC model is a circle of all personality types. You may prefer or be one or more types, but you have other styles in you that you can draw on, or incorporate in your behavior in any situation. You may have to think about it and work at it, but you can do it.

As you read more about the DiSC, you may read that certain styles make better salespeople, or teachers, or leaders, or whatever. The truth is, those are all stereotypes. The most successful person in any role is a person who has a deep understanding of themselves and can draw on each of the styles within them. The DiSC is just another way to help you understand yourself, your goals, your motivations, and the way you engage with and influence others. DiSC is about how you can establish and maintain rapport with your clients and others.

Building Rapport

I think of rapport as an acronym: really all people prefer others reflecting themselves. People like themselves. They like people who think, talk, and act like them or understand them. When you can show someone you care, understand, and think like them, you're immediately a step closer to a relationship with them, to a sale, and to being a successful salesperson. Adapting to someone's communication style is not about manipulation. It's about being willing to communicate on someone else's level. Successful salespeople do the following:

- Build rapport with people fairly quickly

- Communicate with people the way they prefer to be communicated with

- Communicate on the client's level if they want them to even consider buying from them

- Develop the attitude of a teacher or educator, not a salesperson

You build rapport when you develop mutual trust, friendship, and an affinity or bond with someone. Rapport feels like having a connection. You "click" with the person. Rapport is a tool for building relationships and more. It's the foundation of success. When you have rapport with someone, they're more likely to want to help you succeed, and vice versa. When you have rapport with someone, you're in a better position to influence them. You're more likely to learn from and teach each other. As the trust you build with this person grows, other people they know and influence will be more likely to accept your ideas, to share information with you, and to create opportunities together. All that grows out of rapport.

Rapport isn't trust, but it's closely related to it. Rapport focuses on establishing a bond or connection. Trust is more about establishing a reputation for reliability, consistency, and keeping your promises. When you have them both—you're golden.

Not all of us learned how to make friends or create rapport growing up. Fortunately, it's never too late to learn.

Learn and remember people's names. There's nothing sweeter to any of us than our own name. Learn people's names and use them. Don't overuse them, but when you're introduced, repeat their name. Use it in a sentence. For instance: Someone introduces me to their friend John. I say, "John, good to meet you. So, John, how do you know _____," (the person who introduced them). This helps me associate John with the person who introduced us. Before leaving the conversation, use their name again, and when you say goodbye, say something like, "Good to meet you, John," or "John, I'm looking forward to hearing more about _____." If they give you a business card, write down a sentence or two on the back about where/how you met. Include some information about them, a pet's name, or a favorite hobby they may have mentioned, to help you remember them and where you met, and what you talked about.

Be culturally appropriate. It's almost impossible not to offend someone for something these days. The person may be any age, gender, faith, background, or from any walk of life. You won't escape offending everyone, but try to be culturally sensitive. And if you screw up, apologize sincerely and humbly, then move on.

Smile. There's a Russian proverb that translates, roughly, to "laughing for no reason is a sign of stupidity." Russian culture doesn't encourage smiling, but American culture definitely does. If you're not able to crack a genuine smile with people they think something is wrong with you. Fake smiles don't work. They're worse than no smile. If you have to stand in front of a mirror to practice a warm, genuine looking smile, do it. Smiles build rapport.

Relax. No one likes to be around tense people. If you're tense because you're worried about what others are thinking about you—stop. No one is thinking about you as much as they're worrying about what you're thinking of them.

Do What Your Mother Told You. All those things mothers say, like "Hold your head up," or "Don't slump, stand up straight." or "Pull your shoulders back," are good advice. Show people you feel confident by maintaining a good posture.

Listen. For a lot of people, listen to others means keeping their mouth shut until they can jump in with their own opinion, ideas, or story. True listening means you can hear what a person says, and understand what they said thoroughly enough to repeat it back to them in a way that they feel they were heard. This can mean listening to what is not said as well as what is said. Learn to listen. Studies show that people find those who listen more than they talk as more fascinating and friendly. People who feel you've heard them won't remember what you said but rather *how* you made them feel.

Don't overstay your welcome. If you've *clicked* with your prospect you will feel excited, connected, and eager to learn more, hear more, and say more to this new person. Don't. Say goodbye and walk away. Leave people wanting more of you, not less. This can be tricky, but pay attention to their body language to observe signs that your prospects are becoming restless. Make sure you don't dominate the conversation.

There are hundreds of books on building rapport, but all of them require you to get out and practice what you're reading and learning. I suggest checking out some MeetUp groups (https://meetup.com) that will put you in front of potential buyers, Toastmasters where you can develop your speaking and presentation skills, or social groups in your area where you can practice your rapport-building skills.

11

Follow-Through

"Knowing others is intelligence; knowing yourself is true wisdom. Mastering others is a strength; mastering yourself is true power."

—Tao Te Ching

This chapter is very short. Why? I want to *introduce* rapport building to you. I could write a full book and create an entire course on the subject of follow-through. I will do this in the future, but for now I want to provide you with some foundation and *start the conversation and instruction.*

So, let me begin with this timeless truth:

Selling is more than just a sale. It is about selling over time—reselling, up-selling, cross-selling, and more. It's about constantly nurturing your relationships with key prospects, clients, and even strangers you meet who have the potential to become prospects or clients. And, like all relationships, clients must be nurtured, fed, and maintained. Closing the sale is only the first step to creating a lifetime of repeat sales. Your follow-through is what will ensure the trust you've worked so hard to create is maintained.

Think about the last time you went to a really nice restaurant with a great server. You know, someone who knew exactly when to stop by your table and ask how the food was, or who anticipated your need for a drink refill or other services. Remember how it made you feel to know you were being taken care of and your needs were met? It made the meal and the experience so much more enjoyable. Now think about a time you were ignored, your drinks weren't filled, you had to flag down your server to get your check, or wait on some items from your order to be delivered. That's how powerful or annoying the right amount of contact with your client can be. Anticipate their need for a follow up after the sale. If they haven't bought from you, follow through:

Set up a time for your next contact (Call, leave a voicemail, then send a follow-up email) with them.

Ask them if they have any questions or concerns. Wait two weeks. If they don't respond, go through the exact same steps again. Keep your messages short, sweet, and to the point. Send them some type of white-paper that *shows* them your expertise. Then, make another phone call. Make them tell you "yes" or "no."

The truth is that most people don't follow up enough. Be persistent until they say "no" or "don't bother me." Let them know you don't want to waste their time or yours if they're not interested. If they say no, accept it gracefully, thank them for their time and interest, and add them to your cold list. Your "cold list" is a potential gold mine if you understand selling.

During the many years I built my sales expertise and then mentored and coached others in successful process, I realized that most people in sales stop one or two personal touches before a sales is made. It's the person who understands that, today, everyone is distracted with the constant information we are all bombarded with daily.

So, it truly is the person who stays centered and committed to consistently and thoughtfully connecting to prospects that is the one to not only *secure* the sale but also *sustain* the sale. Think about the fact that if you show your targeted prospects that you are a good person and that you will also be a good vendor partner for them. In other words, look at your consistent outreach as a demonstration of your steadfastness. Just make sure that when you go through the steps I suggest above that you follow through again and again.

This step is the epitome of *selling from the soul*. Embrace it for all it offers—a positive and richly purposeful way to create relationships that will last.

12

The Real You

"We are constantly invited to be who we are."

— *Henry David Thoreau*

Being your true, authentic self at every opportunity helps you become a better entrepreneur, leader, and human being. Being real can make you better, but being real isn't easy. We're not encouraged, especially the men of my generation, to be vulnerable or show our emotions. As children, we're taught not to be authentic, not to be real, and not to be vulnerable because people will use us, manipulate us, or hurt us.

Entrepreneurs especially don't see the value in being real. They believe, as I did, that even if your business is circling the drain and you're worried about making payroll that you should put on a brave face and appear strong and confident to the people around you. There's a time and place for that, and I'm not saying let everyone see you sweat.

I'm saying that authenticity breeds trust, and trust breeds business. When you learn to be real, to be your authentic self, you'll have the confidence, wisdom, and awareness you need. You'll know that all you need is in you now. You'll know you don't need to wait to "become" successful. You are successful. You are enough. When you find out who you are, you will be able to program yourself for success.

Here's how to start:

Your Internal Reality

All you need is in you now. Don't just read that and nod. Read it and meditate on it. Write it down in your journal. What does it mean? Who are you right now in this moment?

Begin to develop "I am" statements. You may have heard these described as "affirmations" and shrugged them off, or said, "That's never worked for me." Here's the thing. Affirmations do work. Affirmations have the power to program your mind into believing whatever you tell it. The reason why affirmations don't work for some people is the negative affirmation, the existing thought pattern the person already has, is so strong that it cancels out the positive affirmation.

Make Your Affirmations Work

Affirmations work best if you can first identify the negative or unhelpful belief that is keeping you stuck. Maybe your parents always told you that you wouldn't amount to much, or were fat, or lazy, or stupid. Maybe you grew up hearing you were ugly, or dumb, or incompetent. These negative thoughts can be memories of hurtful things others said to you or things you think about yourself. Maybe you didn't make a sports team, or get that chair in band, or make all A's and you told yourself you weren't talented or worthy. Step one in creating effective affirmations is writing all those negative thoughts down. Your thoughts can include your qualities. Here's what you do:

Make a list of what you've always thought of as your negative qualities. This can include your finances, your looks, age, personality, intelligence, or athletic or musical abilities. Yes, it's painful. We don't want to think about these things, let alone write them down where someone else might read them. But do it. It's a critical step in creating positive affirmations that will change your life. Speak this negative thought or affirmation out loud and notice where in your body you feel uncomfortable as you say it. You may notice pain, or a heaviness, some muscle tightening, or just discomfort in some part of your body (head, chest, arms, legs or hands). This is where your body is "storing" that negative energy or thought.

Create an affirmation that contradicts the negative affirmation you just wrote down. Maybe you wrote, "I'm fat and out of shape." The opposite of that is, "I'm healthy, fit, and the perfect weight for my height." Use the strongest, most specific words you can. If you're not sure if the words are strong enough, ask your spouse, a trusted friend, coach or mentor for feedback.

Say the affirmation out loud for at least five minutes, three times a day—morning, midday, and evening—while looking in a mirror. Yes, look at yourself when you're saying this! Write the affirmation down on an index card or sticky note and place it somewhere you can read it throughout the day—your bathroom mirror, the dashboard of your car, computer monitor—wherever you're likely to be able to glance at it and read it. Memorize it. Speak it out loud when you're driving, waiting on hold on the phone, or walking.

As you start speaking your positive affirmation, place your hand on that part of your body where you felt discomfort when you spoke the negative affirmation. Breathe your positive affirmation into that part of your body.

Start asking questions of yourself. Get to know *you*. The quality of your life is dependent on the quality of the questions you ask yourself.

13

Now What?

"Warning: the brain resists change. It takes the brain between thirty and sixty days to get used to a new situation or, in this case, a new belief.

If you regress during that time, you often have to start again. Your results are often determined by the beliefs you hold. Create a map of design, not default.

It's never too early or too late to start making positive changes in your life."

xc Tao de Haas, psychotherapist, social ecologist, corporate trainer

We've covered a lot of things in this book. Here's a recap of what I've shared in hopes you'll take action on them. Changing our lives requires consistently acting on what we learn. I don't want to sound like a sports coach here, but then again, I do. Without a desire for influencing people, you're not going to get far or do well in sales. Desire is a sense of longing or hoping for a person, object, or outcome—like a craving. When you desire something or someone, you get a longing for that thing. You're excited by the enjoyment or the thought of the item or person, and they want to take actions to obtain their goal.

One of the things that I do want to say here—as I say in most everything—is take what you can use. For the rest of it, if you don't understand it or don't like it, don't use it. I'm convinced that most people get information overload with anything that they listen to. Even if you're trying to become better initially, too much information can overwhelm you which can make you give up. In a way, it's like creating capacity. You get overwhelmed and broken. Rather than trying to do it all at once, parse it out and find the things you can digest, understand, and apply. Then go for it.

The main thing is to keep it simple. Don't overcomplicate and overthink this. You can probably use 80 percent of what I'm giving you in one shape or form eventually. You might not use it all now. You won't ever use 100 percent. The things that I've listened to from the best people in the world that do what they do have impacted me, but I don't use 100 percent of what I've learned.

For instance, years ago, I listened to a series that was based on a study that came out of Stanford University where they studied the psychological profiles of the top salespeople they could find; the top one percent of the top one percent were in the study. They asked these people questions and developed a series around those questions and answers. They came up with the top twelve things these people continued to master. I can tell you that the information in it was unlike anything I'd ever heard before. Each of these twelve teachings was like listening to a dictionary a day. If you listened to two of them in a day, it was like reading an encyclopedia. It was overwhelming.

I've listened to the entire series many times over the years, and I've used some of it and some of it I haven't used. Some of it I wasn't comfortable with. Some of it just wasn't my style or personality. Some of it never fit with my personal beliefs. That doesn't matter. My point is, I don't care what you pay attention to, or who you follow, or what mentoring you're getting from books like this or talks or different events that you go to. It's all wonderful—for someone.

However, if you can't use it and it doesn't fit you, just put it down. Pick it up in the future and it might be useful then. Shelve it. Write it down and put it in a file where you can go back and look at it again. Take notes and go back and read your notes. Start a journal as you read and study different things. Every leader—anyone who has ever changed their world, or the world—keeps a journal. If you want to grow and change, start journaling.

If you want something that can help you change your business life as far as learning day by day in a system, have a journal just for the business side of your life. I intermingle all my journals. I write in two or three, sometimes about business, sometimes about life.

I learned this about fourteen years ago and I've been journaling since then. For fourteen years, I've journaled my sad times, my good times, my bad times, and my mad times. Journal everything. When you go back and read what you've written, you'll find that there's a lot of wisdom and insight in things that you said then that you don't see until long after the fact. When you see how upset you were, then look at the outcome, your perspective changes. It will give you strength for the future.

Books, Mentors, and Thought Leaders

A lot of people judge a book, CD, podcast, or video by how much information they get out of it. The more, the better they think. I believe if you can get one or two insights or techniques out of a talk, a book, or a program, it's a good book, talk, or program. Why? Those insights add up over time. If someone comes to you with a word, advice, or a suggestion that helps you, it's a good word. You don't need to hear twenty pieces of advice before that one piece is "good." You never know what you're going to find in a book or CD that strikes a chord in you. Your friend or co-worker may find nothing in a book, because it doesn't speak to who they are, but you may find yourself reading it every year because it's filled with advice and insights relevant to you. Be open.

I'm going to give you the names of a few people I admire and have learned from over the years. I've listened to and followed a mentor of mine, Lance Wallnau, for several years. His writings on business and on putting things together is world class. Tony Robbins is another person I've never met, but whose teachings have had an impact on me. He makes the statement that repetition is the mother of skill. In other words, skill comes through repeating a process, learning from it, receiving feedback, and moving on.

My top five books have changed over time, but one of my current top five is *Daring Greatly* by Brené Brown. It's really a wonderful read. *The Gifts of Imperfection* is another of her books I like. It's not quite as long as *Daring Greatly* and it explains things more simply. You can also check out her TED Talks about authenticity and vulnerability.

John Maxwell's *21 Irrefutable Laws of Leadership and Failing Forward* and Napoleon Hill's *Think and Grow Rich* are must reads. There's some information in *Think and Grow Rich* that doesn't necessarily apply directly to sales, but I like a lot of the material. There are many good tools in those books.

If you're going to influence, you should read Dale Carnegie's writings—*How to Win Friends and Influence People* is a great start.

Some books will be life altering. *The Magic of Thinking Big*, by Dr. David J. Schwartz, long regarded as one of the foremost experts on motivation, was one of my life-altering reads. This book will help you sell better, manage your life and business better, earn more money, and—most importantly—find greater happiness and peace of mind. *The Magic of Thinking Big* gives you useful methods, not empty promises. It's a book that changed my friend's life in the early 1980s. I read it and it set me on the course where I'm at today, making this series. Hopefully what I'm sharing will help change and give others insights about how to be better at what they do as well.

I've read James Allen's *As a Man Thinketh* dozens of times since I first read it in 1983. I still have the marks and the highlighted parts that stood out to me then. I like keeping older books that I can mark up and make notes. If you read on an iPad or a tablet, that's fine. But there's some value for me in having an actual paperback that I can write notes on and go back and reread.

If you journal on your computer or another device, I think that's wonderful. You don't need to have a physical journal, but I like writing on real paper when I'm journaling. My wife types her journal on her Mac. There's no right or wrong way to journal. I just want you to find a way that you can do it that will allow you to retain and save the information, so you can go back and read it over and over again.

I've compounded one journal that has *life statements*. I have another with what are called "*I am*" statements that includes some of my *prophetic potential* insights as well. These are basically the three things I journal about now.

Also take time to regularly create your own *life statements*. For example, one might be, "Let learning and breathing end simultaneously." That's a life statement for me. Another one I've created is, "Achievement through personal transformation is the essence of life." The things and thoughts that burn inside you, change you, and create pivot points in your life are the things you should be documenting. They can be your creations or they can be statements from someone you admire. Harvest those these statements putting them where you can regularly go back and read them again and again. Don't worry about how well the ones you create read. They are for you, not for publication. The more you write, the better your writing will become. Just write and write and write your own statements regularly.

Experience and Excellence

There are some practical tools you can use to develop your skills—any skills. Skill is developed through repetition. You can't just repeat something; you must repeat it correctly, meaning that if you have a lousy pitch, repeating it a thousand times won't make you better. Learning to pitch correctly, getting a good pitch, and then repeating it a thousand times will develop your skill. Basketball legend Michael Jordan put it this way: "You can practice shooting eight hours a day, but if your technique is wrong, then all you become is very good at shooting the wrong way. Get the fundamentals down and the level of everything you do will rise."

This is why I emphasize excellence and experience. Without excellence, experience means nothing. Without experience, you'll never be excellent. They're two sides of the same coin. The reason I tie experience and excellence together is that in Proverbs it says, "See a man excellent in his business, he will stand before kings."

Excellence in something is what gives you an audience at a high level, but excellence is built through experience. Experience begins when thoughts spring up inside of you that turn into thought, then theory, then actions. When you have thoughts about something, and then formulate a theory, and you believe and have faith that that theory will bring forth the results you want, then you take action. Action brings forth result, and then you have an experience.

Many times, the result or experience you get isn't the one you were going for. How many times have you thought about a business and put a plan together because you thought, "Man, this is going to be great. I'm going to make this work." You took action and the result you got was pitiful. Or worse, you completely failed. That experience, bad as it might have been, was the feedback. Don't see it as a failure. Even if the results were nothing like you wanted, see the experience as a success.

Why do I say that? Because in every failure, there is feedback that will provide information you need to have success down the road. Everything is beautiful in its own time. Believe that. Have faith that everything you learn, everything you experience, everything you do, and every time you fail is a gift. You may not see it immediately, but it's there. That's another reason why you journal—so you can see that happen. That will develop your faith and belief in the process as you see how much you learn and grow and succeed with each perceived failure.

A lot of times, your ideas, your theory, your thoughts, your experiences, and the excellence you're trying to gain fail because of timing. If you take the right step, but the timing is wrong, you'll probably fail. It's like the economy, which runs in a cycle that usually goes five, seven, eight years up and then two years down. It almost mimics the stock market: bear and bull. If you're in an economic upturn in the first couple years and you can see it and can feel it, then you know there's typically another three or four good years in front of you. If you hit the gas there and you take more risks, you're going to like it. If the economy is dipping and you hit the gas, you're not going to like it. I've taken risks and tried to do things when the economy was dipping. Being young and not knowing these cycles, I got hurt. In business, if you hit the gas when you should hit the brakes, it's going to hurt really bad. That's my point. That's just a good analogy.

I'm not saying don't take risks. Taking risks and actions is what gives you experience, and experience is what gives birth to excellence. That's the point. Experience and excellence are tied together. You won't have excellence without having a lot of experience. That's why Lance Wallnau says that it takes sometimes twenty-five years to create an overnight success.

My question to you is: when are you going to get started? You're probably thinking, "I can't take twenty-five years." I tell you that those twenty-five years are going to pass whether you're doing anything or nothing. You can choose to act or not act. Either way, in twenty-five years, you'll be twenty-five years older. Do you want to also be twenty-five years wiser and more experienced? Then start acting now.

I want you to get this. If you need to close ten sales a month to sell whatever you're selling, and most of the people in your group get six or eight appointments a day, and out of that six or eight, they're able to close an average of ten or more a month, what do you need to do to close more? Just think about that. Six or eight, five days a week.

I know an individual who decided that if everybody in the business who is closing ten to twelve sales a month and they're setting up six to eight appointments a day to get to that point, the best salespeople must be doing something different. That was his thought. He looked at the best salespeople, the ones who were closing the most. He developed a theory. He decided that he was going to get in front of twelve to fifteen clients a day. Think about that. Let's say the average salesperson got six a day and he got twelve. Basically, he's seeing double the number of people in a day that the good salesmen were seeing.

In a matter of a year—fifty weeks, to be exact—he saw six more people a day, which is thirty more people a week. Thirty times fifty means he was seeing 1,500 more people a year. He was getting more appointments in a year than their top salespeople. With those numbers, he closed more sales than anyone else. Think about that. The average salesperson was seeing 1,500 people a year, while he was seeing 3,000. He got two years' experience in one year. This is what I'm saying about experience and excellence and how they're tied together. He thought, he took action, got feedback—experience—and then he got a result and learned how to bring forth excellence.

So, you can say, "I don't want to take twenty-five years to be an overnight success," or you can say, "I want to get experience faster, so I'll take more action, learn from it, get the feedback, and then move again and get better." Take the feedback and get better because that feedback will help you develop the skills. Remember: "He who is excellent in business, he will stand before kings." Excellence comes through practice. Period.

Again, Michael Jordan says it best: "Be true to the game, because the game will be true to you. If you try to shortcut the game, then the game will shortcut you. If you put forth the effort, good things will be bestowed upon you."

You may not know that Jordan didn't make his high school basketball team the first time he tried out. He was pissed. A classmate he didn't believe was as talented or as good as he was made the cut. But he didn't let that thought or his failure stop him. He put in twice the time, learned twice as fast, and became a better player than he imagined he ever would. Yet, he kept failing throughout his career. He said, "I have missed more than 9,000 shots in my career. I have lost almost 300 games. On twenty-six occasions, I have been entrusted to take the game-winning shot—and missed. And I have failed over and over and over again in my life. And that is why I succeed."

Go practice all you need to. Learn all you can. When you have an experience, receive the feedback, gain more understanding and skill, and go again. Set some goals for six months out, and twelve months out. Find out how many people you need to see, how many sales you have to close. This is why you journal. This is why you keep up with stuff, and why you need to know your numbers, your failures, and your successes. If you can't measure something, you can't manage it. When you start selling, write down how many people you're seeing a day or a week and how many you're closing. Do this consistently, religiously. Don't skip a week. You're only cheating yourself if you miss this step.

You're not going to close more than 20 to 25 percent unless you're a superstar. You might eventually be that. I was. At one time, I closed up to 40 percent, but I owned the business that I was closing in, too. I had a very high level of belief and faith. That 40 percent closure rate didn't happen overnight, by the way. It came through the very steps I gave you: thought, theory, action, result, experience.

Each time I went out and failed, I brought back more excellence. So, there's your plan: if you want to get ahead faster, work harder. Instead of taking five years to reach your goals, you need to see more clients, so it takes you two years. It's really simple. Experience, when you receive feedback and make adjustments from it, will lead to excellence.

That's it. In a nutshell: Be authentic. Fail. Succeed. Journal. Learn. Grow. Treat your clients the way they prefer to be treated. Track your successes, but study your failures because that's where the golden nuggets to your future success lie.

As I've said throughout this book, in one way or another, success in sales is all about success in relationships with the people around you. It's about how much of an influencer you can become because you care about people. That's what this book is all about: heart and soul. Once you grasp the truth in that, not just the head knowledge of the concept, but the emotional, mental, and spiritual wisdom of it, nothing can hold you back from success in selling.

Wait! There's One More Thing!

I would be remiss if I didn't offer you the opportunity to really take the lessons you have learned in this book to *the next level*. To this end, please visit my website at www.donwlong.com. There you will find a wide array of tools to help you keep up your learning and mastery of *selling from the soul*.

From my heart to yours, here's to your success!

Don W Long

Acknowledgements

I'd like to begin with a very special thanks to my three girls, the greatest gifts of my life. To my wife, Cindy, your belief in me is only surpassed by The Creator Himself. I love you. To my daughters, Ashton and Jordan, who have always encouraged me to pursue the desires the Father put in my heart and have been an inspiration to me to keep becoming the best I can be. Love you both so much.

To my friend, Owen Hurter, who inspired me to write this book over a cup of coffee. Thanks, Owen, for your belief in me. A very special thanks to all the creative people who worked hard to make this project possible. Thank you to Michelle Kulp, my publisher who also provided extensive book coaching and publishing support. Thank you to Becky Blanton, my writer and editor. And thank you to Josh Smith, cover designer and website creator.

Finally, I want to give a special acknowledgement to my first sales mentor, Larry Takacs. Over thirty-five years ago, Larry taught me the basics of sales and led me to truly sell from the soul. Thank you for mentoring, inspiring, and guiding me through the beginning of my sales career.

Can You Do Me A Favor?

If you enjoyed this book or found it useful, I'd be very grateful if you'd post a short review on Amazon. Your support really does make a difference. I read all the reviews personally so I can get your feedback and make this book even better.

Thanks again for your support!

Don W. Long

End Notes

[i] J. D. Meier, "Don't Confuse Strengths and Weaknesses with Skills," *Sources of Insight,* http://sourcesofinsight.com/strength-and-weakness/.

[ii] J. D. Meier, Getting Results the Agile Way: A Personal Results System for Work and Life (Bellevue, WA: Innovation Playhouse, 2010).

[iii] Bruce Duncan Perry, "Respect: The Sixth Core Strength," *Scholastic,* http://teacher.scholastic.com/professional/bruceperry/respect.htm.

[iv] Cynthia Bazin, "Nine Traits of Trustworthy People," *Success,* November 26, 2015, https://www.success.com/9-traits-of-trustworthy-people/.

[v] Emotional Intelligence Test, *Psychology Today,* https://www.psychologytoday.com/us/tests/personality/emotional-intelligence-test.

[vi] Michael Akers and Grover Porter, "What Is Emotional Intelligence (EQ)?" PsychCentral, https://psychcentral.com/lib/what-is-emotional-intelligence-eq/.

[vii] Stephen Joseph, "Seven Qualities of Truly Authentic People," *Psychology Today,* August 26, 2016, https://www.psychologytoday.com/us/blog/what-doesnt-kill-us/201608/7-qualities-truly-authentic-people.

[viii] People First Productivity Solutions was founded in 2006 with the goal of helping companies boost productivity through people development. See https://www.peoplefirstps.com/about_us/.

[ix]Deb Calvert, "Research Reveals What Buyers Value—It's Not What You Think," March 2008, https://blog.peoplefirstps.com/connect2sell/what-buyers-value.

[x]"Frank Abagnale," *Wikipedia*, https://en.wikipedia.org/wiki/Frank_Abagnale.

[xi]"Business Ecosystem," *Investopedia*, https://www.investopedia.com/terms/b/business-ecosystem.asp.

[xii]"Wolf Reintroduction Changes Ecosystem," *My Yellowstone Park*, Jun3 21, 2011, https://www.yellowstonepark.com/things-to-do/wolf-reintroduction-changes-ecosystem.